JINKY . . . NOW AND THEN

Jimmy Johnstone is one of the most colourful and controversial characters in the history of Scottish football. In a career spanning 14 glorious years, "Jinky", as he was affectionately known, was the outstanding personality in a Celtic team which brought the European Cup to Britain for the first time. His amazing dribbling ability was appreciated around the world by fans and opponents alike. At his peak the wee man ranked alongside greats of the game like Best, Law, Cruyff and Eusebio. He was an entertainer and showman with a unique gift, a man described by his big hero and pal George Best as "a genius who could walk into any team in the world". But there was another face to Johnstone, one which landed him in hot water with club and country. In *JINKY . . . NOW AND THEN*, Johnstone relives the good and bad times of a career which took him from humble beginnings in Uddingston, Lanarkshire, to Celtic Park – where his heart is to this day. For the first time Scotland's greatest winger speaks frankly about the man he admired above all, Jock Stein, and the shattering grief he experienced when the Big Man died. He shares the joy of Lisbon, 1967, when Celtic defeated mighty Inter Milan to lift the European Cup, the torture of Argentina and the World Club Championship and the fear of Madrid on the night his life was threatened in 1974. The wee winger has his say about the Scotland fans who made his life hell at Hampden and recounts the true facts behind the infamous Largs rowing boat incident which rocked Scottish football and robbed him of a taste of the World Cup Finals. He makes his private life public and talks openly of his blackest day, in June 1975, when Celtic gave him a free transfer, before taking a critical look at what's happening behind the scenes today at Parkhead. Johnstone also pulls no punches on the part "bevvy" played in his life and the valuable experience he gained working on a building site after the glory years had gone. But through it all this enigmatic character has retained a sharp sense of humour and *JINKY . . . NOW AND THEN* is punctuated with tales and anecdotes from a true comedian. But more than anything it is the life story, warts and all, of a footballing legend the like of whom we may never see again.

JINKY
...NOW AND THEN
THE JIMMY JOHNSTONE STORY

JIMMY JOHNSTONE
AND
JIM McCANN

MAINSTREAM
PUBLISHING

First published in Great Britain in 1988 by
MAINSTREAM PUBLISHING COMPANY
(EDINBURGH) LTD.
7 Albany Street
Edinburgh EH1 3UG

ISBN 1 85158 153 7 (cloth)
ISBN 1 85158 154 5 (paper)

British Library Cataloguing in Publication Data:

McCann, Jim
    Jinky — now and then.
    1. Scotland, Association football
    Johnstone, Jimmy
    I. Title II.
    796.334′092′4

    ISBN 1-85158-153-7
    ISBN 1-85158-154-5 Pbk

Cover colour photograph by Jeff Holmes.
Jacket design by James Hutcheson.

Typeset in 11/12pt Times by Pulse Origination, Edinburgh.
Printed and bound in Great Britain
by Billings and Sons, Worcester.

DEDICATION

To my lovely wife Agnes, children Marie, Eileen, James and grand-daughter Emma who are my number one team. This book would not have been possible without them.

ACKNOWLEDGEMENTS

With special thanks to Tommy Thomson whose help was invaluable in the preparation of this book. Thanks also to Jean Stein, George Best, John Greig, Ian St John, Jim Baxter, Bobby Charlton, Denis Law, Bobby Lennox, Sean Fallon, Ronnie Simpson and Pat Woods. Pictures courtesy of the *Daily Record*, *Sunday Mail*, *Daily Mail*, *Daily Express*, *Glasgow Herald*, *Evening Times*, *Celtic View* and photographer Jeff Holmes. Over the years many people have helped me on and off the park. Some are mentioned within the pages of this book but thanks also to the following: Tam McCluskey, Joe Connor, Frank and James, Tommy McDonough, Peter Quinn, Mike McCabe, John Devaney, Sammy Cairey, John Stonnie, John McDade, John Chisholm, John McCafferty, the "Mason Boys": Ian, big Alex, wee Alex, John McPherson. All the staff at the Windmill Arms and manager Dennis and wife Yvonne. John Mullen, John Gavin, Danny Logan, the Brandons, Irish Mick, Corry, Jim McCormick, John Baxter, Cathy, John McEnernan, John Carlin, Jimmy McNeill (Billy's father) and to anyone else who knows me.

CONTENTS

Foreword

by Jean Stein

No one gave my late husband more problems off the pitch and more pleasure on it than Jimmy Johnstone.

Celtic FC was Jock's second home and he treated all the players like family. But Jimmy was unquestionably his favourite son because despite all the rows — and there were many — Jock thought there wasn't a bigger talent in the game than the wee man.

Off the field both Jock and I had a deep affection for Jimmy and his wife Agnes and family. For my part Jimmy was and still is a charmer, a lovable character with no badness in his soul.

To Jock he was a temperamental genius. If he was alive today my husband would be generous in his praise for one of Celtic's greatest players. For me he summed up Jimmy's worth as a footballer with these words a few years ago: "People might say I will be best remembered for being in charge of the first British club to win the European Cup or nine championships in a row, but I would like to be remembered for keeping the wee man, Jimmy Johnstone, in the game five years longer than he might have been. That is my greatest achievement."

THE ENTERTAINER

Jinky . . . as others see him

For more than a decade Jimmy Johnstone captivated the football world with his unique dribbling skills. At his peak the wee man they nicknamed "Jinky" was a world-class performer who could be ranked alongside greats like Eusebio, Cruyff, Best and Charlton. With the majestic Celtic teams of the late 1960s and early 1970s he won honours galore, including a European Cup winner's medal. But a footballer can gain no higher honour than the admiration of his peers and in the compiling of this book there has been no shortage of that.

GEORGE BEST . . . "Jimmy was different class. One of the few players who brought the fans in and kept them in. He was a great entertainer and showman who always wanted to give the fans value for money. If he beat three opponents he would want to beat another three and usually did. Simply marvellous to watch. Without doubt the wee man was world-class. A genius with the ball and a real character on and off the field. A very special player indeed."

BOBBY CHARLTON . . . "At his peak Jimmy was a fantastic little entertainer with superb close control. He was almost impossible to dispossess. A world-class performer. I will always remember a match at Newcastle when Jimmy played for the Scottish League against the English League. He ripped us apart that night. Even Sassenachs had to stand back and admire a little magician at work."

11

IAN ST JOHN . . . "Jinky was an apt nickname for the wee man with a style all of his own which allowed him to 'jink' past defenders at will. One of the game's greatest entertainers. A truly world-class performer in the years when Celtic swept all before them. It's one of life's mysteries why he won only 23 caps for Scotland. It was the country's loss."

JOHN GREIG . . . "Everywhere I go people complain about a lack of personalities in the modern game. Jinky was a great personality and the older I get the more I appreciate how good he was. Every time he got the ball you expected something to happen. The wee man didn't just beat opponents, he gave them a roasting. On his day he was as good as anyone in the world. People got the wrong impression when we faced each other. If the ball was there to be won both of us, as good pros, would go for it — and Jinky usually lost in one way or another! I'm glad to say we are still good friends. Jimmy was a great wee character and a tremendous entertainer. I always admired him."

JIM BAXTER . . . "I've not been to a game for over four years but I would go back tomorrow if Jimmy Johnstone was still playing. One of the best players I've ever seen — only Best was better in Britain. Jimmy could do anything with the ball. I'm convinced it was tied to his boot at times. Despite being Old Firm rivals for years, I admired Jimmy's ability immensely. The world will never see another Jinky . . . more's the pity."

DENIS LAW . . . "Jimmy was one of the most naturally gifted players ever to grace the game. His unique dribbling ability allowed him to beat defenders almost at will. Fans loved him and even opponents admired his magical skills. A world-class entertainer in the Stanley Matthews mould. In my opinion there will never be another Jimmy Johnstone. A born genius who was also full of fun off the park.

Chapter One

THE BIG MAN

A part of me will never accept that Jock Stein is dead. The "Big Man", as everyone in football knew him, was a genius, the like of which the world will never see again.

I remember vividly the night he died back on 10 September 1985 after Scotland had drawn 1-1 with Wales at Ninian Park, Cardiff, in a crucial World Cup qualifying tie. I heard the news of his death at my home in Uddingston around 11 p.m. after a telephone call from an old Parkhead buddy, Bobby Lennox. I just couldn't believe it. Someone very special to me had been snatched away, never to be returned. I was devastated. The great man who made the Lisbon era and Celtic's ensuing years of glory possible, was gone.

Jock's funeral at Linn Crematorium was an ordeal for myself and all the ex-Lions. We were united in grief at the passing away of our father figure. Even today I still think about the Big Man and sometimes I feel he is watching me from above. Occasionally, while I am sitting in a pub having a quiet drink with friends, I half expect the phone to ring and there, on the other end of the line, is Jock — tracking my every move just like the good old days!

It has been well documented that I had my run-ins with the Boss and I will recall some of those occasions later in this chapter. But I can't say a bad word against Jock. He was the biggest influence on my football career. He could have crucified me (and boy it felt like it sometimes) but instead he made me into a star.

In my opinion Celtic should erect a monument to the Big Man at Parkhead in this special year. Everyone connected with the club owes Jock a tremendous debt of gratitude and it would be tragic if he was not given his proper place in the history of Celtic — right at the top of the pile. Honestly, if I had the spare cash I would do so myself. Jock lifted Celtic out of the doldrums and put firmly in the past the dark days when they were also-rans in Scottish football. But he did much more than that. Under his unique influence the club was elevated to a lofty place in the annals of world football. Without him they might still be chasing shadows.

He certainly cast a magic spell over me right from the start. I remember the first time I experienced his power back on a cold January night in 1965. The Big Man had already been appointed the new manager of Celtic in succession to the great Jimmy McGrory but the official announcement was delayed until March, when he eventually stepped into the manager's chair. So even the players did not know the news at this stage. I was playing in the reserves at Parkhead, ironically against Jock's team at the time, Hibernian. At half-time, with the score 0-0, I was relieving myself in the toilets when the Big Man breezed in. Over the years I was to learn that Jock's biggest asset was his ability to motivate players. He had the uncanny knack of pressing the right button. Anyway, this night he turned to me and said: "What are you doing out there, wee man? You should be in the first team." I was having a stinker up to then but, for some reason, his words lifted me and I proceeded to bang in a hat-trick in the second half.

From that moment on I was under Stein's spell. Of course it wasn't all sweetness and light between the Big Man and myself. As everyone knows, for a wee man I had a rather big mouth which often worked overtime. I will never forget the time when it almost put my neck in a noose.

It was back in October 1968. By this time Celtic had been deposed as kings of Europe after losing to Dynamo Kiev in the first round of the Champions Cup after the Lisbon campaign. But we were on the march again the following season in Europe and a crucial tie with the crack French outfit St Etienne lay in prospect.

Three days before the second leg we faced Dundee United in the league at Parkhead and I was having another stinker. The Boss, quite rightly, decided to pull me off in the second half. No player ever likes to suffer the indignity of being substituted but, unfortunately, I lost the rag. As I came off to make way for George Connelly I shouted abuse at Jock in the dugout and threw my strip at him on my way up the tunnel.

Within seconds, I heard the sound of heavy feet chasing after me. It was Jock and he sounded like a bear with a sore head. For a caused further uproar by saying that, in future, I would devote all my energies to playing for Celtic and I no longer wanted to be considered for international duty. That in turn was smoothed over and I did play for Scotland again as you will read later.

A month after the Dundee United debacle Stein once again proved to be the master motivator for yours truly. We were playing Red Star Belgrade in the second round, first leg, of the European Cup at Celtic Park and it was 1-1 at half-time. There were 67,000 fans at Parkhead to see Bobby Murdoch give us the lead but the Yugoslavians equalised before the interval.

Now, my fear of flying is legendary but this night Stein, the wily old fox, used it to Celtic's advantage. He came into the toilets (a lot of important business was carried out there) and struck a bargain with me, saying: "Jimmy, if we win by four clear goals tonight I will let you miss the second leg in Yugoslavia." That was enough for me. I didn't fancy another trip in a "big bird" so I grabbed the game by the scruff of the neck in the second half and turned in one of my best performances for Celtic, scoring twice and making another two for Bobby Lennox and Willie Wallace.

Don't ask me how I managed it. It must have been divine intervention. In the last few minutes, with a 5-1 lead, I was back in our own box clearing everything in sight. I remember Billy McNeill telling me in no uncertain terms to get up the park. "No chance, pal," came the retort from this exhausted individual. Of course Billy and the rest of the boys were bemused. Jock hadn't let them into our secret pact.

I'm glad to say he kept his promise, although not before trying another fly move. The following day Jock called me into his office and explained that he had received an approach from the Red Star coach virtually begging him to play me in the second leg. "They want to see the great Jimmy Johnstone in Belgrade," said Jock. "You can't let them down." But I wasn't wearing it and Celtic qualified without my help in the return.

That is a well-known incident but there have been other less public occasions when Jock kept me in check and I will always be grateful for his helping hand. Needless to say "bevvy" landed me in bother with the Boss, who was a strict teetotaller.

One Saturday we had just won a league game at Parkhead against St Johnstone and I was in a hurry to get away for a pal's stag night. Out of the blue Jock announced that he wanted us to report to Celtic Park the following day for extra training. Now training on a Sunday was unheard of and there seemed no real reason for it. We didn't have a midweek game. What puzzles me to this day is

Two greats together. Matt Busby presenting the BBC's team of the year award to Jock Stein, the best manager of all time.

whether it was a massive wind-up by the Big Man. Did he know I was going out on the town for a skinful? Was it purely a cosmetic exercise aimed at catching me out?

I duly sped off and got well tanked up that night. In the morning when I woke up it felt like a band was playing in my head. I was still half sozzled. I knew I was cutting it fine to make it to Celtic Park on time so I pulled on the same clobber I had worn the previous day and, as luck would have it, hitched a lift to the ground in a pal's bread van!

By the time I reached H Q I was breathing a little easier. Of course, in my tender state, I had forgotten that the clocks went forward the previous night, marking the end of British Summer Time. I was an hour late! Jock spied me right away and obviously clocked I was under the weather. I was caught red-handed and red-faced. He approached me and said sternly: "You, get changed and get up that bloody terracing and stay there until I come back for you."

For the next half an hour I ran up and down the steep stairs at the

Pleased as punch after being honoured by the fans.

Rangers end nursing an almighty hangover. The rest of the lads thought it was a scream but I felt more like throwing up!

I'm convinced Jock could hear the grass grow. He certainly had an almost sixth sense which told him where I was at any time of the day or night. He proved it again on another famous occasion during pre-season training. In those days we trained in the mornings and afternoons during the summer. Bobby Murdoch and I liked a quick shandy or two in between sessions so we slipped off to my little local boozer, "The Noggin" in Uddingston. It was the era when the pubs shut at 2.30 p.m. so it was always a race against time to quench our thirst. This particular day we were sitting comfortably at the bar when the telephone rang. The barman approached me and said: "It's for you, Jimmy." I was mystified. No one knew where I was, or so I thought.

No second guesses who was on the other end of the line. "You two get back here, pronto." It was the Big Man, on the ball again. That's why I said earlier that even today I get the impression Jock is watching as I down a pint or two!

But, despite his public image as a stern disciplinarian, the Gaffer had a tremendous sense of humour. He loved nothing better than to sit with the lads having a laugh and a joke. Even when the pressure was on he could floor us with his wit.

I recall a time when we were preparing for a big European tie at our favourite retreat in Seamill on the Ayrshire coast. Jock was in the middle of one of his famous, brief tactics talks. He spent little time talking about the opposition but on this day it was just too long for me — I was desperate for the loo. So I put up my hand and asked to be excused. The Boss didn't bat an eyelid as I departed. As I reached the door I heard him say to the rest of the boys: "We may as well keep going. That little bugger never listens to me anyway. He just does his own thing."

That was another great thing about Jock. He gave me a free role. He knew there was little point in filling my head with tactics. My big strength was being an individual and taking players on all over the park.

People constantly ask me what was the Stein secret. How did he make us champions of Europe? I can only say that he did the simple and logical things superbly well. He instilled self-belief in his players. It may sound all too simple but the man was a genius. He sussed people out in two minutes flat. Many times, when we took on highly rated and highly paid Italians or Spaniards, we would be standing in the tunnel before a game while the opposition strutted around with their film star looks. They would stare at us —

The Kelly Dynasty. From left, Desmond White, Sir Robert Kelly, Tom Devlin and Jimmy Farrell.

and what a sight. Wee Bobby Lennox and I with only a few teeth and old Ronnie Simpson, looking like a Muppet with no teeth at all! But Stein had pumped an inner confidence into our veins and, sure enough, within 20 minutes the Italians had faded and their tongues were hanging out as the Lions roared.

Talking of Italians, I must mention another classic moment when Jock displayed his wicked sense of humour. It was shortly after Lisbon and we were men in demand. One day the Big Man received a call from a representative of AC Milan. He quickly relayed a message over the Parkhead intercom asking me to come to his office. When I arrived he said: "Wee man, I want you to hear this." Milan were tabling a bid of £100,000 to lure me away from "Paradise". Quick as a flash Jock replied: "£100,000. That's a lot of cash for just one game." Suffice to say the man from Milan was bid "arrivederci" in double quick time. Moments like that confirmed my belief that, underneath it all, the Boss thought the world of me.

I was undoubtedly more of a problem to him than his own children and he must have felt like kicking me from here to kingdom come sometimes. But there was a mutual admiration between us, something I will treasure to my dying day. Off the park Jock helped me a great deal. He could sense if I had little domestic problems and, more often than not, he would come to my home and play a part in sorting them out. He wasn't sticking his nose into private matters. The Big Man treated his players like family. He believed if they had troubles away from the game it could affect their performance on the park — and nothing was allowed to come between Celtic and success.

This dedication to duty almost postponed my marriage to my lovely wife, Agnes! It was back in 1966. I was a member of the Celtic party which embarked on a 35-day, 20,000-mile tour of Bermuda, the United States and Canada during which we played 11 games — winning eight with three draws and no defeats. It was a hectic tour and near the end players started falling like ninepins with injuries. The situation was getting pretty desperate with two games left when myself and full-back Ian Young were both due to fly home to get hitched to our respective partners. True to form, Jock tried to persuade me to stay on. The night before I was due to jet back to Scotland he pulled me aside and said: "Wee man, I'm struggling. Don't go home yet. We need you. Can you not put the wedding off for a week?" I stood firm although often I regret the decision.

Don't get me wrong. I'm not having belated second thoughts about my marriage. It's just that my famous fear of flying started on that fateful trip. The flight home was a nightmare. We took off from Toronto but within half an hour the plane ran into a huge air pocket. The aircraft dropped like a stone. It was horrific. Plates, glasses, crockery and luggage flew all over the place. A young American sitting next to me bashed his head off the luggage rack and bit through his tongue. It was his first trip, as well. I was squealing like a banshee while holding on to poor Youngie for dear life.

It seemed like an eternity before the plane suddenly steadied itself. Later, the pilot told us that a similar incident had happened the year before but the plane ploughed into the Rockies on that occasion, killing all passengers. What an escape we had. From that day I didn't want to board another plane although I did, of course, in the line of duty.

I thought long and hard about cancelling our honeymoon in Majorca but eventually relented. Who knows? Maybe the Big Man saw it all coming! Maybe it was his way of warning me again. I wouldn't put it past him.

Seriously, I owe a great part of my life to Jock Stein and his wife Jean who has kindly written a foreword for this book. Jock stood by me through thick and thin and made the greatest moments of my football career possible.

Jimmy in full flight

Chapter Two

LISBON

Locked away in a bank vault is my most treasured possession — a European Cup winner's medal from Lisbon, 1967. I could never bear to lose that little piece of gold. Just touching it brings memories flooding back of the unforgettable evening of 25 May in the stunningly beautiful Estadio Nacional when a band of home-grown Scots conquered Europe at their first attempt by beating mighty Inter Milan 2-1.

Stories of Celtic's greatest triumph are now part of Scottish football folklore. But I must let you in on a little secret — I thought it would never happen. I honestly felt we were in for a thrashing! Obviously I kept this to myself at the time but I'm pretty sure other members of the team felt the same way.

Inter's reputation at the time was enormous. OK, it was a reputation built on defensive strength. It was unattractive and boring but it had twice won them the European Cup, in 1964 when they defeated the incomparable Real Madrid and the following year when they saw off Benfica of Portugal. They had also won the World Club Championship and the man guiding them, Helenio Herrera, was the world's highest-paid coach. Jock Stein had shown us videos of them in action and, privately, I believed Inter were invincible. I remember thinking on the way to the game: "If this mob score first we've had it."

Looking back, maybe it was just pre-match nerves which made me imagine the worst. Big Jock certainly didn't promote negative thinking. He had done his homework right down to the last minute

Celebration time again during the Lisbon era as the League Cup is safely back in our possession.

detail and he even mastered the devious Herrera in the pre-match propaganda war.

Our confidence could not have been higher. We had made a clean sweep of the domestic honours, winning the League Championship, Scottish Cup, League Cup and Glasgow Cup — an achievement I feel no team will ever match. And in Europe we had overcome stiff opposition. In the first and second rounds respectively we disposed of Zurich of Switzerland and the Frenchmen from Nantes. The hardest nut to crack was, undoubtedly, Vojvodina of Yugoslavia in the quarter-finals. The Slavs inflicted our only defeat of the Lisbon campaign, winning the first leg in Novi Sad 1-0. That set up the sensational second leg at Parkhead two weeks later. Stevie Chalmers levelled the aggregate score early in the second half. And then, with the seconds ticking away and a play-off at a neutral venue in Europe looming, big Billy McNeill popped up in the last minute to head home a Charlie Gallagher corner. There has rarely been a finish like it at Parkhead. Truly astonishing.

The Czechs of Dukla Prague stood between us and a fairytale place in the final and that's when Willie Wallace proved his worth. Shrewd Stein had captured "Wispy" from under Rangers' noses earlier in the season for a record £30,000 from Hearts and he grabbed two goals on his European debut to give us a 3-1 first leg win over Dukla in Glasgow. Yours truly netted the other goal, incidentally.

Prague is supposed to be a beautiful city but I saw little evidence of this on our short trip. The stadium was eerie. The place looked as if it was haunted. And to make matters worse Celtic, for the first time in my experience, played a defensive game to grab a 0-0 draw. Still, the end result was a place in the European Cup final so we were all over the moon. But Inter, I thought, would be a different kettle of fish. That was until I saw the thousands of Celtic supporters who had travelled to Portugal.

They were, and still are, different class. Many must have begged, borrowed or stolen to make the trip. We hadn't seen very much of them in the lead-up to the game. Naturally, we needed peace and quiet so our base was the magnificent Hotel Palacio, just along the coast from Lisbon in the scenic millionaires' paradise of Estoril. But as our coach sped towards Estadio that afternoon we passed hordes bedecked from head to toe in green and white. I recall thinking at the time: "We must bring the Cup back to Glasgow for their sake."

Maybe the omens were in our favour that day. May 25 is the feast of Corpus Christi, a holiday of obligation, so all the Catholics in the team went to mass on the morning of the game. Assistant manager Sean Fallon stood in as an altar boy because the priest had been left in the lurch. (Sean would do anything for a drink of wine!)

The first thing I recall as we stepped on to the pitch was the heat. It was over 80 degrees and I felt sticky and tight throughout the game. But here and now I will say that many of the Lions were disappointed with their performances on that day of days. I have certainly performed much better. Two men, though, excelled themselves in the final — Bobby Murdoch and wee Bertie Auld. They were immense and in my opinion this duo did more than anyone to ensure our place in history. Bertie and Bobby showed the millionaire Italians a thing or two about class, especially in the early minutes when Celtic ran all over Inter.

Thankfully after those early exchanges I rid myself of any inferiority complex. Inter didn't seem like the supermen I had imagined. So even when Jim Craig pulled down striker Cappellini in the seventh minute and referee Kurt Tscheschner of West

Celtic coach tours. Another bus trip for the lads.

Germany awarded Inter a penalty from which Sandro Mazzola scored, I felt we were a match for the Latin aces.

History records that big Tam Gemmell bulleted home an equaliser in the 62nd minute and Stevie Chalmers popped up to deflect a low shot from Bobby Murdoch home for the winner six minutes from time. But what it can never tell me is how many goals we would have scored if Inter had come out of their defensive shell. I'm sure we would have murdered them!

Herrera's highly paid henchmen had no answer to our attacking flair. They were methodical. We were magical. I will never forget their man-to-man marking. It was, and still is, the most frustrating tactic to counteract. The highly rated Burgnich tracked me all over the place. It didn't matter about the ball. He just followed me. The guy rarely made a forward run or a decisive pass. His job was purely to police Jimmy Johnstone. I'm sure if I had popped off for a quick half and a beer — and in the heat it was an appealing idea — Burgnich would have been at my back. Inter were masters of the containing game but for the first time they had been found out by a bunch of working-class boys, a large percentage of whom hailed from Lanarkshire coalmining families.

Strangely enough, I bumped into Burgnich only a few years ago at Parkhead when he was in Scotland on a spying mission for an Italian team. Now, his English rivals my Italian so we only managed to exchange a few words . . . nicer ones, I hasten to add, than on that evening in Lisbon.

Harking back to Lisbon, I remember feeling numb when the final whistle sounded and all hell broke loose around me. It wasn't the feeling I had expected. Sure, all the boys jumped around and the fans flooded on to the pitch as we raced for the dressing-rooms. But even after I had the Cup in my hands it did not sink in that we were the best in Europe. Throughout the post-match banquet and the flight home I was in a daze.

When we touched down in Glasgow I thought there had been a nuclear holocaust. The streets were deserted. But when we hit London Road I could see why. Every Glaswegian seemed to be packed into that little pocket of the city — 60,000 men, women and children were waiting at Parkhead to salute the champions of Europe and we paraded the Cup to the people who matter most, the punters.

I was speechless. Now that was real emotion, a night I will never forget: at "home" with those fantastic fans. When the euphoria died down I rushed back to my real home to be with my wife Agnes and all the family and friends. Sadly Agnes could not be with me in Lisbon because four days before the final she gave birth in Calderbank House Maternity Hospital to our first child, a lovely daughter we named Marie. What a lovely way to round off the greatest week of my life, by holding my new-born baby in my arms.

Marie was joined a year later by Eileen and then James, who is now a teenager. So I have a small team of my own. But on the football field there will never be a team to match the Lisbon Lions. They were unique.

But the Lisbon era wasn't just about the players. Parkhead was a special family. Everyone from the groundsman and the backroom boys up to the directors and chairman had the club at heart. The chairman's wife Lady Kelly, Jean Stein, Wendy Fallon and other board members' wives contributed to the unbeatable atmosphere.

Some of the characters were priceless and I'm glad to see some are still around at Paradise and I class them as personal friends. Jimmy Steele, the club masseur, is one example. He was, and still is, a real joker in the pack. Jimmy would keep our spirits up in far flung places by regaling us with tales and giving us his own special brand of opera. After one note you knew he wasn't a regular performer at Covent Garden but his wailing was wonderful. They

A dream come true as we show off the biggest pot of the lot.

Two amigos celebrate our Lisbon success and the Big Hombre hopes the bottles are empty.

should strike a medal for the man. Jimmy would spend countless hours massaging players and sometimes I felt he had a secret fetish! (Only joking, Jimmy.)

Doctor John Fitzsimmons was another class act. John was a devout Roman Catholic and his first act when we arrived in foreign parts — even behind the Iron Curtain — was to find the nearest chapel. To this day I have the utmost respect for the man. Characters like Sean Fallon, Neilly Mochan and Bob Rooney come into the same category and their names will crop up much later. But to others, too numerous to mention, I say "thanks for everything".

The club was certainly in safe hands at the top. Where could you find more respected men than Sir Robert Kelly and Desmond White? When Sir Robert was knighted in January 1969 it was no

Wee Bertie takes centre stage after our Lisbon victory.

more than he deserved. The man was Celtic through and through. He started the youth policy which was vindicated on that glorious night in Lisbon but before that Sir Robert had to endure a rough ride from supporters who were hungry for success. He was a man of real integrity as he displayed on countless occasions throughout his regal reign at Parkhead.

Sir Robert had his critics who said he was a dictator but anything he did was for the good of the club. His death left a hole at Celtic Park which has never fully been filled. Not many people will know that he shared my fear of flying and always carried a set of rosary beads when we were airborne. The man gave a fortune to charity and never forgave people who criticised his first love, Celtic FC.

I was always one of his favourites at Parkhead. I think he saw me as another Patsy Gallagher, his all-time hero on the pitch. I will never forget his first few words to me shortly after I arrived at Celtic Park: "Jimmy, anything you need just come and see me. My door is always open." That meant more to me than all the money in the world.

Desmond White also loved Celtic passionately although I feel the fans misinterpreted him, especially when he occupied the Chairman's chair. Desmond couldn't hide the fact that he didn't come from a working-class background but he was far from pompous. He gave unstinting service to the club and again he is sadly missed. I remember him telling me that he could not read a newspaper after a Celtic defeat. That's loyalty.

On the park there was no big secret formula for the Lions. Big Jock held the reins like a champion jockey. Football was in the players' veins and he made it flow. We approached every practice game like a cup final. We treated every team with respect and our attitude was always right. Jock wouldn't have it any other way. That helped us in Europe because these were just another series of games which had to be won, in style of course.

The atmosphere among the players was exceptional. I feel that had a lot to do with Jock using only 18 players in that 1966/67 season — and only 15 regularly week in, week out. To the men who played in Lisbon you added John Hughes, Charlie Gallagher, Willie O'Neill and the luckless Joe McBride who missed the European Cup final through injury. Ian Young, Dave Cattanach and John Fallon played only a handful of games but they slotted in perfectly. Consistency of choice certainly worked perfectly because in the Lisbon season we had a record of having played 65, won 53, drawn 8, lost 4. We scored 201 goals and conceded only 50. That will never be matched.

We were such a tight-knit bunch. Even for training games we had two regular sides and the Big Man always acted as referee. Some of his decisions were blatantly wrong but he did this as a wind-up—and it worked.

Religion never entered our minds. I say this because bigotry is still a big issue, particularly in the west of Scotland. In those Lisbon days we had a balanced mixture of Catholics and Protestants and, sure, we would take the mickey out of each other about religion but there was no sectarian nonsense. We had too much respect for each other. Funnily enough, one of the favourite songs sung by the boys on coach trips was "The Sash" because of its melodic tune. There was usually a medley of Irish songs but no rebel tunes.

I count it as a privilege to have played for the club in those days, although maybe I didn't appreciate it at the time. But I'm positive of one thing. There should be a "Hall of Fame" inside Parkhead today to honour the Lisbon men. People may accuse me of living in the past but the memory of those legendary Lions must never die.

Meeting one of the movie star figures of Inter Milan, Facchetti.

Chapter Three

REAL TEARS

As if Lisbon wasn't enough, 1967 also marked another highlight of my life — barely two weeks after our European Cup triumph. The great Alfredo di Stefano, Real Madrid's White Arrow, asked Celtic to provide the opposition for his testimonial match on 7 June at the majestic Bernabeu Stadium. I was overjoyed. Me, little Jimmy Johnstone from Uddingston, playing on the same pitch as a god like di Stefano and all those Real superstars.

It was our first game as champions of Europe and 100,000 fans turned out to see this soccer showpiece. What followed will live with me forever. It was a night I wept with joy. I recall within 15 minutes of the kick-off the match was stopped and all the spotlights turned on di Stefano who left the field to tumultuous applause and made his way up to the Presidential box. The Argentine-born genius seemed to be walking on air but when he eventually reached the top a replica of the European Cup was placed in his hands. The noise was incredible as the fans paid homage to one of the greatest players ever to grace the game. All around me legends like Gento, Santamaria and Sanchez cried unashamedly. I was overcome with emotion and the tears began to flood down my cheeks.

Words cannot fully describe how I felt. Just to be part of such a momentous occasion was a dream come true and I'm sure those scenes inspired me to a performance which had the critics raving. I could do no wrong as Celtic swept to a 1-0 win, courtesy of a goal by Bobby Lennox which was set up by yours truly. Goalkeeper John Fallon was our real hero of the night, denying Real with a string of

Knights of the round table. From left, Willie O'Neil, Bobby Lennox and yours truly.

stupendous saves. I've seldom enjoyed myself so much on the football park before or since and to this day I have a private video recording of the occasion. It is one of my all-time favourite archive tapes.

The night also produced one of those classic funny stories and, surprise, surprise, the comedian was Willie O'Neill. As I've already said, Willie was a true wit. I used to run around with him, Bobby Lennox and Bobby Murdoch off the park and together we had some rare times.

Willie had an answer for everything and it was always delivered with a straight face. One of his pet fears, though, was being "nutmegged" and, as a full-back, Willie proudly claimed that no one had ever managed to put the ball through his legs. Full-backs hate that because it makes them look so foolish. Anyway, there was Willie running alongside di Stefano in front of 100,000 fans when, all of a sudden, the White Arrow slipped the ball through Willie's legs and hared off. After the game the boys mercilessly ribbed Willie with good-natured abuse about the incident. Surely his super-cool front would crack this time, I thought. As quick as a flash Willie retorted: "But there's not many players can say they were nutmegged by an all-time great like Stef." We were left

The great Alfredo di Stefano greets the Celtic party on our arrival in Madrid for his testimonial match in 1967.

speechless. Willie had turned the story on its head and who could argue with him? We all felt 100 feet tall that night.

Celtic's victory over Real rounded off the 1966/67 season and what a record we could hold up for inspection. I'm proud to say I played in 54 games and scored 16 goals as we rose from unknowns to lords of the manor.

But football's a funny game, as Jimmy Greaves is fond of saying, and it has a habit of kicking you in the face at the most unexpected moment. Sadly, that is what happened. The following season didn't start too well for the club or me personally. Because of the withdrawal of an Albanian team, the European Cup holders — who usually received a bye into the second round — were forced to play in the first round. Unfortunately, we drew the formidable Dynamo Kiev who came to Glasgow on 20 September — the day the QE2 was launched at Clydebank — grabbed two goals and shut up shop. We pulled one back near the end through Bobby Lennox but by then we knew we had a mountain to climb in Russia.

Three days later I was sent off against St Johnstone for punching Kenny Aird. It was my third early bath and I was suspended for 21 days (an historic suspension as you will hear later). Worse was to follow on 4 October when we lost our European crown behind the Iron Curtain. The second leg started well with Bobby Lennox levelling the aggregate score. But then the Italian referee sent off Bobby Murdoch for no apparent reason and followed this up by chalking off a second Celtic "goal". To rub salt into the wound the Russians scored in the last minute to the delight of 100,000 comrades.

Celtic were certainly guilty of underestimating the Soviets. Possibly for the first time ever we got too big for our boots. As champions of Europe we thought we had a divine right to progress as far as we wanted in the competition. Despite all our bad luck in Kiev, the tie had been lost in Glasgow. It was a costly lesson but it helped us to learn to always keep our feet on the ground. Could the season get any worse, I thought? Well, the answer was literally only days away . . .

Chapter Four

ARGY-BARGY

The mere mention of Montevideo or Buenos Aires still makes my blood boil. Twenty-one years on I can't forget the savage injustices which took place in those South American "torture chambers". I'm talking, of course, about Celtic's infamous ties with Racing Club of Argentina in the 1967 World Club Championship. It was more of a nightmare than going 15 rounds with world heavyweight boxing champion Mike Tyson. I'm convinced only fate prevented deaths on a football field.

The first leg at Hampden Park on 18 October was like a teddy bear's picnic compared to what lay in store. We thought we had seen it all from Argentinians the previous year when they disgraced themselves in the World Cup at Wembley. But at Hampden they kicked, punched and elbowed their way through the 90 minutes. Their cynicism was disgusting. How Celtic players kept their cool that night I will never know. I finished the match with my hair matted with spit.

Days later I went into the history books as the first player to have a domestic suspension lifted temporarily so that I could play in the return leg. I wish the SFA hierarchy had not bothered!

When we landed in Buenos Aires at the end of October the hostility was incredible. It was like a lynching party and we were the victims. The team and officials stayed at the Hindu Club, a country club about an hour's drive from Buenos Aires. It was more like a hostel than a hotel. On the Sunday night before the game the Roman Catholics in the Celtic party decided to go to mass.

Although it was only 200 yards along the road armed guards accompanied us. That was nothing unusual. They ate, drank and virtually slept beside us!

The journey to the game was hair-raising as hordes of Argentinians clobbered our bus with anything they could lay their hands on. The noise was like thunder.

I certainly got the message when we arrived at the Avellaneda Stadium. A Racing Club official handed me a box and inside, folded neatly, was the strip of the guy who had marked me at Hampden. I assumed it was his way of telling me, "I'm going to get you, pal". Before the game started our keeper Ronnie Simpson was felled by a missile. He was carried off and replaced by John Fallon, whose bravery that night I still admire immensely. Many people have said that Celtic should have withdrawn at that moment but I know better. If we had walked off the park there would have been a riot. Every Argentinian in the ground wanted a war. I'm sure of that. They were in a frenzy. Some of the Racing Club fans even urinated on our small band of supporters from the top tiers of the giant stadium. Well, I've heard of being pissed upon from a great height but that took the biscuit!

It was impossible to play football in such an intimidating atmosphere, although we tried. Tommy Gemmell put us 2-0 up on aggregate from the penalty spot after I had been pulled down. Racing got away with murder as Uruguayan referee Esteban Marino looked on. He disallowed a good-looking goal from yours truly before Rafo and Cardenas gave Racing a 2-1 win. To this day I'm glad Racing won the game, in the circumstances, because if we had lifted the Cup mayhem would have followed.

The Celtic board were split over whether we should compete in a play-off scheduled for 4 November in Montevideo. Chairman Robert Kelly wanted to fly home but Secretary Desmond White and the Boss wanted to play. I don't blame the men for holding different opinions. By then we were all nervous wrecks but I wanted to play just to show that football could win the day.

Unfortunately the play-off in the Centenario Stadium was a joke — but no laughing matter. I certainly got the "treatment" that day. I was black and blue all over but four minutes from half-time my involvement in the game was halted by Paraguayan ref, Rodolfo Perez Osorio. One of the Racing players tried to pull me down by the shirt so I simply stuck out an arm to free myself. Of course the referee saw it differently and I took the long walk. In the meantime the whole cast of *St Elsewhere* were on the park swathing the "injured" Latin in bandages. It couldn't have been a brain haemorrhage, that's for sure.

The history books will tell you that Bobby Lennox and John Hughes were also sent off although Bobby's case was the worst incident of mistaken identity I have ever seen.

But big "Yogi" was a different matter. The Racing goalkeeper had the ball in his arms when John proceeded to punch him in the stomach. Afterwards we got one of the few laughs of the trip when we asked Yogi to explain his actions. "I didn't think anyone could see me," came the classic reply. There were only about 50,000 fans and a cast of millions watching on TV. Nice one, Yogi!

Celtic eventually lost the match 1-0 but that was academic. No one will ever convince me that Celtic could not have stuffed Racing and been crowned world champions — if football had been the game. But the South Americans didn't want to know about sport. Celtic players have taken flak over the years for their behaviour that day in Uruguay and we certainly did go haywire late in the game but any human being would have cracked under that kind of physical and mental abuse. We could take no more and I don't blame any of the lads for losing control. Don't get me wrong, I wish it hadn't happened but it did and we paid a heavy penalty for going to the Argentine. We were robbed of a prestigious title and fined £250 each by our Chairman into the bargain.

I must be mellowing in old age because I find myself defending the referee who disallowed the goal I "scored" that night. In his position, with a tribe of mental Argentinians in the ground, I would have thought twice about allowing it to stand. The people I cannot defend are the English Press. After the battles of Buenos Aires and Montevideo they slagged off Celtic, calling them sore losers. They went to town on us but the following year it was a different story, when Manchester United suffered a similar fate at the hands of Argentinians Estudiantes. On that occasion they branded the Latins "animals" and talked of "poor" United.

Of course now the annual meeting of the champions from two continents is such a hot potato that it is played in a neutral country — Japan. Teams like Ajax Amsterdam and Bayern Munich have only taken part in recent years after assurances that violent conduct would be severely punished.

Jinky's dad.

Chapter Five

FITBA' CRAZY

I've been a Celtic fan virtually since the day I was born back on 30 September 1944, in a small council house in Old Edinburgh Road, Viewpark, Uddingston. Support for the club ran in the family and my late father, Matthew, took me to Parkhead occasionally on a local supporters' bus.

My first memory of watching the men in green and white isn't a bad one. It was October 1957, and Rangers were the opposition in the League Cup final at Hampden. The legendary Charlie Tully, Willie Fernie, Neilly Mochan, Billy McPhail and Sammy Wilson were in the Celtic ranks but they were still underdogs. By the end of a truly remarkable 90 minutes Rangers had suffered one of the worst humiliations in their history as Celtic roasted them 7-1. Unfortunately, I missed most of the second-half goals — scored at the "Rangers end" — because thick fog had restricted my view, worse luck.

Around that time I missed a lot of Celtic games as I slowly but surely pieced together my own path to Parkhead. It's a far cry from Lisbon but the groundwork started at St Columba's RC primary school in Viewpark, the area which is home to this day. Lessons were certainly of secondary importance right from the start — maybe that's why I became a footballer and not a brain surgeon! The first task on a Monday morning wasn't English or Arithmetic, it was picking sides for the week and laying down jackets for goalposts before the "bell" rang. In between lessons I'd be out in the playground chasing a ball with an army of youngsters. Even

More advice from my biggest fan, my late mother Sarah.

darkness didn't stop the steady flow of football. It amuses me today to hear professional players moaning about the amount of football they are expected to play in a season. Did they not play more as kids — I certainly did — without a word of complaint?

With this passion for the game from the age of five it may surprise you to learn that I was more or less forced into the school team! Unknown to me, my progress was being monitored by our headmaster, Mr Milligan, and one of my teachers, the late John Crines. Both men scrutinised the talent from a window overlooking the playground and obviously liked what they saw from this flame-haired tot. Mr Crines asked me to attend trials but I didn't fancy the idea because, at eight, I was three or four years younger than most of the lads in the school team. Surely I would be out of my league, I thought. But Mr Crines, a regular visitor to Parkhead, twisted my arm and I went on to play in a highly successful St Columba's team.

It was a tough introduction to competitive football for the youngest member of the team. One day we travelled to Holytown

Watching the weans and the biggest wean of the lot is holding on to Santa.

to meet Chapelhall Public in a cup final and lost in a real rough-house affair. To make matters worse I was given a hiding by a few of their supporters after the game, presumably for trying to take the mickey out of a Chapelhall opponent. The following week we met the same team at the same place and turned the tables on and off the field by bringing busloads of supporters from Viewpark. Fighting broke out again but this time some Chapelhall rowdies were on the receiving end.

Around that time there was great excitement in my family. My older brother Pat was attracting attention from Celtic, who were due to send a scout to watch him in a midweek game for the Boys' Guild. Pat packed a shot like Tam Gemmell and could give Allan Wells a run for his money. My dad, who was a miner all his life, didn't want his two sons going down a pit and he had high hopes for his eldest boy on the football park. But, unfortunately, Pat never got the chance to show Celtic what he could do. The Saturday before his big test he suffered severe cartilage damage during a game. It was a heartbreaking end to his hopes of a soccer career and my dad, a quiet, unassuming type, was choked.

By now I was a pupil at St John's Secondary, Uddingston, but, more importantly, I had discovered Stanley Matthews. He was my big hero and I wanted to be an entertainer just like the great man who was later knighted for his services to football. I read one of his early books and was transfixed by his dedication even more than his ability. Matthews pushed himself to the limit and I set out to copy him.

As early as 12 I would run about a mile from school, through a park and over a couple of bings, to my home. After dinner I set out rows of milk bottles on the living-room floor and jinked in between them to sharpen my close control. This drove my late mother, Sarah, scatty until one day she could take it no longer. While visiting a downstairs neighbour, Mrs Watt, mum heard the racket above and immediately ran upstairs and confiscated my ball.

I was in deep despair until a few days later when my mum returned to the same neighbour to borrow some sugar. During their conversation Mrs Watt enquired about the relative calm upstairs and mum explained why peace had broken out. I was told later that dear old Mrs Watt persuaded my mother to return my ball saying: "If he's that keen, let him get on with it. Don't bother about the noise. I'm not complaining." It was a great gesture, one I've never forgotten. For the next five years our neighbour turned a deaf ear to my daily three-hour practice sessions. It must have been terrible for her. Mrs Watt is now dead but her children Billy,

Hail, hail, a Celt is here!

Ian, Alex, Jean and Margaret still live in Viewpark and I want them to know how much their mother's words meant to me.

Another part of my daily drill took me back to the school playground where I would knock the ball off a wall, kill it dead, then imagine what to do as opponents approached from all angles.

To vary the exercise I would then trap the ball and move all in one uninterrupted action. Failure to achieve this brought a self-inflicted punishment lap around the playground. Night sessions followed under street lamps where I would practise "shadow boxing" — twisting and turning, beating imaginary men.

Around this time I got my first big break. One of my teachers at St John's, Tommy Cassidy, was a good friend of Celtic winger Sammy Wilson. Tommy had noticed my potential and mentioned my name in conversation with Sammy one day. Soon afterwards I was invited to Parkhead as a ball boy. For the next year I was in the privileged position of seeing my favourite team in action but I wasn't totally happy. I missed playing football and eventually gave up my post and turned out for the local Boys' Guild team.

Shortly after, our Guild travelled down south for an annual fixture in Manchester. My brother Pat, who was married and living in Doncaster, came along to watch. During the match he got involved in conversation with a man called Wishbone who enquired about the little lad with the red hair. Pat explained the situation and then almost fell over as Mr Wishbone revealed he was a scout for Manchester United. A few days later the scout set up a meeting with me and that's where my old friend Frank Cairney, who runs Celtic Boys' Club, stepped in. Frank followed the Boys' Guild everywhere and was a fanatical Celtic supporter. He was the first person to notice and encourage me and, secretly, he harboured a deep desire to see me end up at Parkhead. Frank insisted in attending the meeting with United officials and, to this day, I thank him for doing so.

During the talks Frank pulled a fly move by insisting I was already provisionally signed by Celtic. It was a calculated gamble. United could have checked up but it worked a treat and they left me alone. Within days of returning from Manchester Frank contacted John Higgins, a Celtic scout at the time, and laid it on thick about how United had almost stolen this bright young talent. I was invited in for training on Tuesdays and Thursdays. In between times I built up my strength by training in my dad's old heavy pit boots for half an hour a night at Thorniewood United Juniors' ground close to my home.

But all the sweat was worth it on 7 October 1961, when I turned out for Celtic Reserves against St Johnstone at Parkhead. I was cheered off the park after scoring once and making the other three in a 4-2 win. That night my dreams came true — I signed for Celtic.

I think my father was even more delighted than me when the great Jimmy McGrory asked this 17-year-old to put pen to paper.

Where it all began back in Old Edinburgh Road.

To this day I thank my late parents for helping to make it all possible. Like everyone in the mining community of Viewpark at the time they didn't have an easy life bringing up five children — myself, Pat and sisters Theresa, Annie and Mary — but they gave us all the love in the world. Dad always encouraged my interest in football while mum, a devout Catholic, lit candles and prayed for me every time I took the park. It was a tight-knit family, so much so that my uncle Paddy stayed with us for a long time.

I soon realised that my other "family" at Celtic was much the same. Manager Jimmy McGrory was the father figure. He was a real gentleman; in fact, a finer man you couldn't hope to meet. Everyone respected and admired him for what he achieved as a player but, despite this, the Celtic boss was a very humble man who never bragged about his exploits. Some modern-day managers could learn from his humility.

For the first year I was farmed out to Blantyre Celtic, during which time I won a Junior cap for Scotland. That day I was watched by Jimmy Gribben who worked in the Parkhead boot room but doubled as a scout. It was on his recommendation that Celtic recalled me from the Junior grade and gave me a contract worth about a fiver a week.

"Grib" was a great old pal of mine. He was an extraordinary character who smoked his pipe in the boot room. When a young player asked him for a pair of boots he would often retort: "Do you think you'll be here long enough to wear them out?" Jimmy had a soft spot for me and I owe him a lot for pressing my claim for a call-up.

I made many other friends, too numerous to mention, in my early days. To all of them I say a big "thank you". Undoubtedly, my dedication to the sport helped further my career with Celtic. I took it all so seriously. For the first 18 months I even had a private pact which stopped me going out with girls (and that's a serious sacrifice). Football came before everything else so it was early to bed every night. I did all the right things and sometimes I wish I still had the same approach!

The first blot on my copybook came on 11 November 1963, when I was sent off against Partick Thistle in a Glasgow Cup-tie after a fracas with Ian Cowan. The ref that day was "Tiny" Wharton, a man I was to encounter many times in future years.

Those early days were tough. Gaining a permanent first-team spot was my goal but the competition was fierce. The last few pieces of the jigsaw fell into place with the arrival of Jock Stein in 1965. At the time I was in and out of favour and Spurs

Star pupil winning a schoolboy cap.

You go your way and I'll go mine.

were following proceedings very closely. One day they sent a representative to watch me against Raith Rovers. I was very tense in case Jock might be prepared to listen to offers for my services. He warned me to turn it on and fortunately I played a blinder — Spurs boss Bill Nicholson was told "no sale".

There were many stories linking me with other clubs during my career. It's true Paddy Crerand once approached me and asked how I would feel about a move to Manchester United. But, while it might have made good headlines for the newspapers at the time, deep down I didn't want to wear any other strip. I had found my real home the day I signed for Jimmy McGrory.

It was called Paradise.

Chapter Six

GANGS, GIRLS AND GAMES

Over the years I have lived a double life. With Celtic I flew all over the world, stayed in posh hotels, dined in expensive restaurants and generally received VIP treatment. It was a life of glamour and fame and I was constantly in the limelight.

But back home in Viewpark I was just plain Jimmy Johnstone. Obviously, everyone in the area knew I played for Celtic and Scotland and often congratulated me on my success. They treated me like a friend but there was no star treatment. People didn't fall at my feet or pester me and they respected my right to have a private life just like the next man. That, more than anything, is why I have never strayed very far from this little corner of Lanarkshire where I was born and brought up.

The place holds so many fond memories for me — more than anywhere in Europe, the United States or South America. From an early age the atmosphere in this typical little Scottish mining area won my heart and subsequently no amount of wealth and world fame persuaded me to desert it for more prestigious pastures.

Of course football was my first love as a child but I would like to give you a brief glimpse into my boyhood days off the park. It's a fairly typical tale of a nipper growing up discovering gangs, girls, games and characters — although not necessarily in that order.

One character I can never forget is Brian Lynch who beat me up twice in the one day! Brian eventually became part of a gang at St John's Secondary School which included myself, Henry McGraw,

Puzzled! Jigsaws were never my forte.

John Delaney, Johnny O'Hara and "Bomber" Liddell, who are all still friends of mine.

Now, like a lot of wee guys, I hung around with bigger boys at school as much for protection as anything else but one particular day no one could save my skin. Someone — I would still like to know who — told Brian that "Superman" wanted to fight with him. Incidentally, "Superman" was a nickname given to me by other gang members to boost my ego. Brian accepted the false challenge and duly wiped the floor with me in a playground ringed with eager spectators. But that wasn't the end of my nightmare because, as the victor was walking away, some other anonymous smart Alex claimed that I wanted a return match, so Brian repeated the dose barely seconds after the first beating, leaving me with a bloody nose. Later we became firm friends, I'm glad to say.

That incident came shortly after I had been a victim of the St John's initiation ceremony which was inflicted on all new pupils. And what a sore one it turned out to be. The test was to jump off a wall into a pile of nettles and bricks. Pointless and painful some may say but I took the punishment like a growing man and held back the tears, although only just.

Thinking back, it's amazing how much mischief I got up to in my formative youth. Our St John's gang would spend hours trying to "jump the burn", a self-explanatory exercise which usually ended up with a cold casualty running home stinking and soaking to his mother.

Thankfully, before we caused ourselves lasting damage, teacher Tommy Cassidy took the gang under his wing. Tommy formed a PT team and took us to shows and gala days all over Lanarkshire. Two nights a week we sharpened up our fitness at Tommy's house. I suppose it was my first real taste of training. Sometimes we would put on three displays in one day and even then I loved the applause of a crowd.

But, as if one gang wasn't enough, I joined another out of school although this one consisted purely of neighbours in Viewpark. Now I hasten to add, despite my beating from Brian Lynch, gangs didn't fight a lot in those days. They were normally just a vehicle for a bunch of boys to run around together. And what a bunch it was in Viewpark. For the first time ever in print I must mention the other members of the Viewpark mafia: Alex and Patrick McMichael, Pat and Robert Green, Tom Gallagher, Eddie Dougan, Robert Moffatt, Billy Donald, Ian Watt, the Murphys, the McLaughlins, the Burkes, the Goldies and the Cairneys. We carried out daring deeds like stealing turnips, apples and

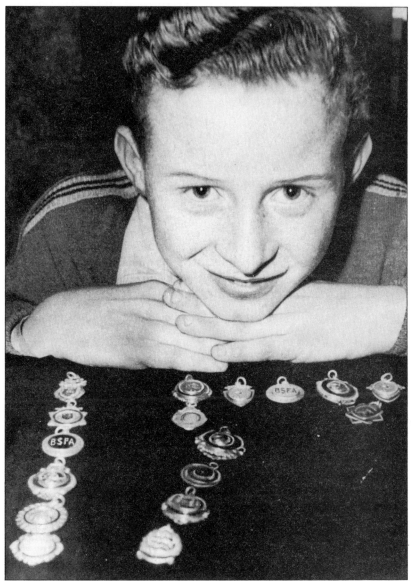

Sweet and innocent Jinky shows off his boyhood medal haul.

strawberries from local gardens. Our playground was Bairds
Avenue, a proper lovers' paradise, where we rudely interrupted
necking couples by playing "cowboys and indians", "kick the can",
"chase the man", "go a plunder" and other adventure games.

Today I rarely see children playing games on the streets. Society

Far from the madding crowd.

has changed for the worse and many parents rightly keep their kids indoors or close at hand for fear of attack. Back in the 1950s Viewpark was just a glen punctuated with strips of houses. It was a tight-knit community where neighbours adopted an "open house" policy which ensured a steady stream of visitors. No one was made to feel like a stranger. Out on the streets a dozen or so boys would be playing "headers" while girls milled around.

Girls certainly posed some problems for me when I was still at school. Being small I felt I had to show off more to attract female attention. Once I challenged three guys to a fight at the same time just to impress a group of girls standing nearby. Although I didn't disgrace myself the young ladies were not impressed and walked off — some guys have all the luck!

On leaving school I started work at a Glasgow meat market carrying sides of meat to the hook but I didn't fancy that as a career so I took a job in an Uddingston clothing factory. After work I dashed across fields to my home in Old Edinburgh Road and grabbed some tea before catching a bus to Parkhead for training with the rest of the ball boys.

While training with Celtic I started an apprenticeship as a welder which involved attending day-release classes but that ended quite abruptly after I had a row with one of my teachers. Both of us were rolling around on the floor when fortunately Benny Rooney, son of the Celtic physiotherapist Bob, pulled me off the teacher. My employer was informed of my misconduct and gave me the choice of concentrating on work or football. Obviously I chose football and packed in the job.

Of course that decision changed my life but it did not wreck my lifestyle. Even today a lot of the same, slightly older, faces are still around me, men like Alex Goldie and John Smith. During my early days with Celtic I took up shooting as a hobby. Alex supplied me with guns. What he didn't know about guns wasn't worth knowing. And John took me on rabbit-hunting and ferret-hunting expeditions to Ayrshire whenever I had time off.

I value their friendship and the same goes for people like Jimmy McNally, Joycie Gallagher, George Delaney, Bill Gilfillan, Bernard Corrigan and Sammy Wilson who still live in Viewpark.

Often I make nostalgic trips from my house in Birkinshaw, which is barely a mile from Viewpark and just as friendly, back to the Old Edinburgh Road house where I lived with my parents. I stand looking at a bannister which I used to "dreep" off on to the road wearing old-fashioned, black sandshoes which offered no protection against the painful impact.

And I think back to the days of the parochial hall discos where I met my wife Agnes for the first time back in the early 1960s. I can't remember if it was love at first sight but I do recall one difference of opinion we had right from the start. Both of us were crazy Beatles fans but Agnes liked John Lennon while I was a true Paul McCartney devotee. But we agreed to differ on who was the best and married in 1966. My best man that day was Eddie Clements, who is still a good friend.

A year after our marriage we moved out of Viewpark and into Birkinshaw to a lovely bungalow which I named "Estadio" after the scene of Celtic's greatest triumph the same year in Lisbon. Marriage gave me an extended family and another set of "parents". Agnes and John Docherty were two of the nicest people I've ever known and have been sadly missed since their deaths. The same can be said for my wife's oldest brother Pat, who tragically died of a heart attack and oldest sister Sadie who is also deceased. But the rest of the family, James, John, Norman, Kevin, Brian, Katherine, Anna and Maureen still visit us regularly in Birkinshaw.

My new home, which I moved into in 1977 after a spell with Dundee, is just a few minutes away from Greyfriars Monastery, a

Wedding day bliss; one appointment I didn't miss.

place which has been my secret sanctuary for the past 15 years. It is run by Benedictine brothers and is so peaceful and private. Over the years if I had problems on or off the park I would sit down at the monastery and contemplate far away from anyone. Even today I train regularly in the grounds. As a Roman Catholic, I also attend confession at the monastery before having a chat with the brothers. One brother spent two years in a Chinese prison for refusing to denounce his faith. I admire him immensely and the same can be said for any person who strongly believes in a particular religion. I certainly believe in God and in Heaven — although I don't think I'm a candidate to join the angels on high when my time comes! Maybe it would be a different story if I could rewrite a few chapters in my life.

One organisation which has changed part of its past is the Royal Oak Celtic Supporters Club in Viewpark. And in doing so they almost moved me to tears. A few years ago I had a call from their president who said the Celtic supporters wanted to rename the club after me in recognition of what I had done for the area. I was overwhelmed. It was one of the most satisfying moments of my life to be honoured by my "ain folk".

Chapter Seven
FEYENOORD FOUL-UP

Losing a cup final is something every footballer dreads. The feeling of having come so far to fall at the last hurdle is indescribable. I have experienced the "emptiness" of such occasions but none can compare with 6 May 1970, a date which still haunts everyone connected with Celtic Football Club. The scene was the daunting San Siro Stadium in Milan. Celtic were overwhelming favourites to win the European Cup for the second time. Only the dark horses of Feyenoord from Holland stood in our way and Glasgow was gearing itself for a night of celebration to rival the scenes which followed our historic victory in Lisbon three years previously.

Over the years a thousand post-mortems have been held into what went wrong on that disastrous date when the form book was turned upside down and Celtic's name was tarnished as a new era dawned for Dutch football. The popular belief is that Celtic players were more concerned with making money than winning the Cup. Countless stories have stated that we worried more about bonuses in the lead-up to the game than anything else. Even Jock Stein has been blamed for not doing his homework on the opposition.

I want, once and for all, to knock these tales on the head. There is one reason and one reason only why Celtic failed to lift the European Cup in Milan . . . *overconfidence* on the part of the players.

To justify my case I must explain the background to that fateful occasion when Celtic went down 2-1 after extra time. Seven of our team — myself, Gemmell, Murdoch, McNeill, Wallace, Auld and Lennox — were survivors from Lisbon and we were still household names around the world. Only a month before we had comprehensively beaten the great Leeds United in the semi-finals, a tie which was dubbed the "final before the final". Holland still wasn't rated as a strong football nation despite the appearance of Ajax Amsterdam in the 1969 final, which they lost 4-1 to AC Milan. We were the stars and Feyenoord made up the supporting cast. It was a straight reversal of Lisbon when Inter Milan were the established force in the eyes of the world and Celtic could only be classed as underdogs.

Money never entered into it. Sure the players wanted to make as much cash as possible second time around but we were completely satisfied with what was on offer. A business agent had been appointed and in the lead-up to the game we thrashed out a generous deal with Celtic. In no way did this distract us from football.

Jock Stein had watched Feyenoord and briefed us on all possible dangers. The Big Man left nothing to chance. But footballers are funny animals. No matter what you tell them, they make up their own minds about the task ahead. And, quite simply, we had written Feyenoord off. All we had to do was go out on the San Siro pitch and pick up the Cup. It was a "doddle". The hard work had been done when Leeds were beaten at Hampden Park. We wanted to win for the 20,000 fans who had followed us to Italy and we assumed the script could not fail.

Feyenoord, unwittingly, fuelled our arrogance. As we walked to the dressing-rooms before the game their players stared at us and you could almost feel their admiration. They recognised each and every one of us. It was like Lisbon all over again, except this time we were being treated like gods.

The match was one long nightmare. No Celtic player rose above mediocre and every Feyenoord man played out of his skin. They chased every ball while we chased shadows. Men like Van Hanegem and Hasil controlled the middle of the park and our defence was always under pressure.

Against the run of play we took the lead on the half-hour through Tommy Gemmell but still we couldn't snap out of our complacency and two minutes later Rinus Israel equalised. Our second-half performance was even worse and God only knows how we managed to take the game into extra time. With only three minutes left we were hanging on desperately for a replay which would give us a second bite at the cherry when the inevitable

*Surprise, surprise as 'Lemon' buys a round and, far right, Mafia man
Macari takes the orders.*

happened. A high ball into the box was handled by Billy McNeill
but before referee Concetto Lo Bello could award a penalty kick
Swedish internationalist Ove Kindvall poked it past Evan
Williams. There was no way back for Celtic and when the final
whistle sounded I dropped to my knees. Tears flooded down my
face.

Our overwhelming arrogance had backfired and Feyenoord, the
team from nowhere, had pulled off one of the greatest shocks the
European Cup is ever likely to see.

The nightmare continued after the match. We tried to escape as
quickly as possible but, because of a strike at Milan airport, our
flight was delayed. The place was in chaos with devastated Celtic

fans milling around in a state of shock. A meal was laid on for us but because of the strike we had to eat in the basement. The players were depressed and on the flight home hardly a word was spoken. Naturally, there was no welcoming party at Glasgow Airport. The players drifted home. I wanted to hide my head in shame, privately, back in Uddingston.

Gutted is an overused word in football circles but it aptly describes my feeling after the Feyenoord foul-up. We had let the fans down badly and that was unforgivable. I was almost non-existent at the San Siro. An early ankle injury didn't help my cause. This was inflicted by a big bloke called Laseroms, the hardest player I encountered in my career. He took no prisoners as others, who also felt the weight of his tackles, will testify. He was certainly on a par with my other toughest opponent, West German full-back Bertie Vogts. Wee Bertie was quicker than Laseroms and almost impossible to shake off. During a game he constantly let you know he was there. Both these guys are certainly not on my Christmas card list!

My despair over the Feyenoord debacle reached its lowest ebb a few days after the final when I gave my runners-up medal away to a young friend, Kathleen McCormick, who worked with the *Celtic View* at the time. Tragically, Kathleen died of cancer a few years ago in Dublin and her sister returned the medal to me but to this day it is a worthless memento of a European Cup campaign in which two ties stand out for different reasons.

The first came in November 1969, when we were drawn out of the hat along with glamorous Benfica of Portugal. It meant a nostalgic trip back to Lisbon for the second leg. Three days before the first game at Parkhead we captured the League Cup, defeating St Johnstone 1-0 with a goal from Bertie Auld. That set us up nicely to face the Portuguese who boasted stars like Eusebio, Coluna, Torres and Simoes. Goals from Tommy Gemmell, who had slapped in a transfer request after being left out of the League Cup final team, Willie Wallace and Harry Hood gave us a commanding 3-0 lead to take to Portugal.

Celtic prepared for the return match at the Hotel Palacio in Estoril, our headquarters before the final with Inter in '67. But this was much more than a trip down memory lane. It turned out to be one of the longest nights of my life! The great Eusebio breathed fresh life into Benfica with a goal shortly before half time at the magnificent Estadio da Luz but we were still on easy street, or so we thought. A second goal midway through the second half put us under extreme pressure and when Benfica equalised in the last

Little and Large. Me with keeper Gordon Marshall.

minute we could hardly believe it. Celtic had thrown away a three-goal lead and now had to face a harrowing period of extra time. No more goals were scored so it came down to the toss of a coin to decide which team would go into the quarter-finals. I will always remember referee Van Ravens leading our captain Billy McNeill and the Benfica skipper into another room to do the dastardly deed. It seemed like an age before our dressing-room door burst open and Billy flew in with his arms in the air. He had called right and we were through. The boys went daft, hugging and kissing each other. We knew we had come so close to going out. It was hard not to feel sorry for Benfica that night. Tossing a coin was no way to decide such a crucial tie and later, of course, penalties were introduced — although that's another agonising story for Celtic fans.

Celtic disposed of Italians Fiorentina in the quarter-finals, winning 3-0 at Parkhead and losing 1-0 in Florence. That set up two monumental ties against Leeds which, Lisbon and di Stefano's testimonial apart, gave me my most memorable moments in football.

Without doubt I had one of my greatest ever games in the first leg at Elland Road on 2 April 1970. At that time Don Revie's team were on everyone's lips. They were one of the finest forces in the modern game. Strong at the back, creative in midfield and deadly up front, they boasted names like Billy Bremner, Norman Hunter, John Giles, Alan Clarke and Mick Jones, not forgetting my opponent Terry Cooper, possibly the best full-back in Europe. It was the "Battle of Britain" but the arrogant English Press had written us off before a ball was kicked. No team could live with Leeds, they claimed. Well, we certainly made a nonsense of that statement. A George Connelly goal after only 40 seconds at Elland Road gave us a 1-0 victory. But we completely outplayed Leeds that night. We were absolutely brilliant. I could do nothing wrong and my marker Terry Cooper, who was renowned as an attacking full-back, hardly got over the halfway line all night. Leeds certainly contributed to the occasion. I always thought there was a touch of Real Madrid about them. Maybe it was just the white strips, but they made it an open game.

Honestly, they were the team we had wanted to avoid. We would much rather have faced Feyenoord or Legia Warsaw, the other semi-finalists. But after the first leg our tails were up and 15 April could not come quickly enough. Before this we lost 3-1 to Aberdeen in the Scottish Cup final despite being red-hot favourites. Referee Bobby Davidson — he certainly wasn't a Celtic supporter in his time — did us no favours by awarding the Dons a dubious penalty and chalking off a "goal" from Bobby Lennox.

The build-up to the return game with Leeds and the atmosphere at Hampden on the night when 136,505 fans turned up could not be bettered. Professional players love a big stage on which to perform and they didn't come much bigger than this.

My old pal Billy Bremner levelled the tie in the first half with a hell of a shot from fully 40 yards but, undaunted, we spilled forward and were rewarded two minutes after half-time when John Hughes headed past Gary Sprake. Bobby Murdoch put the tie beyond doubt four minutes later and the scenes at the end were unbelievable with Bertie Auld donning a trilby hat as we did a lap of honour around Hampden. After the game Bremner was quoted as saying, "Celtic were supermen. They are not a team of humans at all." Unfortunately Feyenoord proved otherwise.

That night in Milan was the beginning of the end for the men from the glorious Lisbon era. Stein was already planning ahead and young men like Kenny Dalglish, Danny McGrain, Davie Hay and Lou Macari were staking claims for regular first-team places which could not be ignored.

The following season, in March 1971, we were comprehensively beaten by Ajax in the quarter-finals of the European Cup. The Dutchmen thrashed us 3-0 in Amsterdam and, despite a goal from yours truly in the return at Hampden, Celtic went out 3-1 on aggregate. I was obviously downhearted but I admired immensely the way the Dutch played the game. By then Holland were becoming a potent force in world football and it was easy to see why. Their game was a joy to watch. It was full of attacking flair and gifted individuals who were given scope to express themselves.

Top of the tree was Johan Cruyff. In my book he is right up there with all-time greats like Puskas, di Stefano and George Best. Possibly only Pele was better. Cruyff was such an elegant mover but deceiving into the bargain. His skills allowed him to do something out of the ordinary all the time. Even playing against him was an honour. I couldn't fail to appreciate the grace and poise of the man. Cruyff was the type of player the fans paid to see, much like Diego Maradona today. The little Argentinian is my favourite present-day player. He can do anything with the ball and his mere presence on the park excites the punters.

Near the end of the 1971 season the great Sir Robert Kelly resigned as Chairman of Celtic and Desmond White took over just in time to see the club win the league title for the sixth time on the trot against Ayr United at Hampden. A week later Celtic defeated Clyde 6-1. In any other season it would have been an insignificant game but it turned out to be the last appearance together of the Lisbon Lions team.

Many people still ask me whether the break-up of the Lions was premature. I can see both sides of the coin. The great Leeds team of the early '70s stayed together much longer than the Lisbon legends and maintained a high level of success. Perhaps we could have done the same. But maybe Stein wanted us to be remembered as men going out at the top — not like many boxers, for instance, who attempt comebacks which only tarnish their image. As I've said, Stein, as always, had aces up his sleeves with the emergence of bright new stars. Undoubtedly, youngsters like Kenny, Danny, Davie and Lou learned a lot from us. How could they fail to do so? Celtic were the most successful team in the land and the Lisbon men were always encouraging the babes. But we can't take all the credit. Players like Dalglish had ability which shined like a beacon, even in those early days.

If any youngster wants to model himself on a player then Dalglish is the man. He is undoubtedly one of the modern-day greats. Kenny's attitude was always right — on and off the park. He had fantastic close control and the ability to turn on a sixpence. Like all top-class strikers, he knew where the target was and hit it regularly. Dalglish was also very courageous, a point which is often ignored when people talk about him. He took a lot of hefty knocks but jumped up and kept on playing. I've seen times when his leg was heavily strapped up but he wanted to play. He had a great appetite for football and that made him an extraordinary pro in my book.

Now he is a great manager of Liverpool which, in many ways, is a carbon copy of Celtic. They don't go outside their own doors at Anfield looking for a new boss and I'm sure Kenny has taken a lot of what he learned at Parkhead to Merseyside. There is the same kind of family atmosphere at Anfield as existed at Celtic Park in my day. Kenny was a quiet guy off the park but he had his own mind and that is still clearly evident today.

Danny McGrain was much the same kind of character but he did not have his troubles to seek during a highly successful career with Celtic. Danny overcame a fractured skull and diabetes to become a great full-back for the club and Scotland. He gave 20 years of loyal service to the club but Celtic must also be congratulated for standing by him in the bad times.

Lou Macari was a great wee guy, a real bubbly personality who always had something to say. Every dressing-room needs this kind of character and Lou also did the business on the park, scoring a host of important goals for Celtic before his move to Manchester United. It's also good to see him making progress as a manager with Swindon Town.

Taking a look at the green, green grass of home against Aberdeen at Parkhead.

Davie Hay was the quiet man of Parkhead but, underneath, he had a sharp sense of humour. His move to Chelsea left a massive hole in the Celtic ranks. Davie was as tough a tackler as I've ever seen. I roomed with him during the 1974 World Cup in West Germany when he was probably Scotland's biggest star.

The new breed had certainly heavily infiltrated Celtic's ranks by the time the 1971/72 campaign began. We suffered a shock European Cup first round, first leg defeat going down 2-1 to Bold Club of Denmark but we set the record straight with a 3-0 win in the second leg at Parkhead in September. Later that month Celtic lost a great friend when Sir Robert Kelly died and, on 23 October, Celtic suffered one of their greatest embarrassments — a 4-1 thrashing by Partick Thistle in the League Cup final. It was a day when nothing went right for us and the Jags could hardly believe their luck. Thistle have often been tagged "unpredictable" but never more so than that day.

Despite this body blow we came off the ropes and by March 1972 Celtic had once again reached the quarter-finals of the European Cup. The new boys were firmly established by this stage and I wasn't needed for the first leg. Just as well, because I had a nasty dose of chickenpox at the time! Celtic recorded a famous 2-1 win over Ujpest Dozsa of Hungary in the first leg behind the Iron Curtain. I came off the bench in the second leg at Parkhead and showed there was still life in the "old dog" yet by helping Celtic to a 1-0 win. Lou Macari netted the goal but I was well pleased with my second-half performance. The critics certainly gave me a good write-up.

Unfortunately, Celtic fell at the penultimate hurdle that year in the European Cup. Players hate losing in semi-finals because their efforts are rarely remembered but this defeat, by Inter Milan, was more tragic than most. Celtic had gone to Milan on 5 April and returned with a 0-0 draw. We were just one game away from the final and our fans turned up in their thousands for the second leg at Parkhead to will us to victory.

Inter, just as they had done in Lisbon, packed their defence and we could not break them down — even in extra time — so we faced the agony of a penalty shoot-out. To this day I'm glad I wasn't in Dixie Deans' shoes. Wee Dixie missed the only penalty as Celtic went out 5-4. Everyone was shattered for the wee man. We all knew how low he felt. All players miss spot kicks but what a time for Dixie to boob. He was inconsolable.

Fortunately, Celtic lifted the title for the seventh time in a row on 1 May at Dens Park. Rangers, who had just won the European Cup Winners Cup in Barcelona, finished third — 16 points behind us.

A week later, I'm glad to say, Dixie came out of the doldrums — and how! The fans had been great to him in the wake of the Inter defeat and against Hibs in the Scottish Cup final at Hampden he paid them back with an amazing hat-trick in our 6-1 win. Everything clicked for us on the day against the Edinburgh men who were a formidable force with the like of Pat Stanton, John Blackley, Alex Cropley and Alan Gordon in their line-up. I will never forget Dixie's last goal when he waltzed past a host of Hibs defenders and then beat keeper Jim Herriot twice before netting from an acute angle. For months afterwards the boys teased Dixie in training. "Show us how you did it again," we would say. "I'm bloody sure you couldn't do it again," added some of the lads.

He didn't mind the ribbing — the boot had been on the other foot many times. The ex-Motherwell striker was a great character, a real trickster. He was always up to no good. Sometimes a player would arrive in the dressing-room before a game to find a foot had been cut out of his socks. Sure enough, it was Dixie playing a cruel practical joke. But one time a "funny" rebounded on him

Jinky, jinking!

although, as ever, he laughed the loudest. Paddy McCluskey, another great comedian, was in the bath with the rest of the lads after a game. The boys were clowning around but Paddy sneaked out early and dressed up in Dixie's clothes. As I recall Dixie was going somewhere special that night (he always was) and had worn his Sunday best. But when Paddy reappeared Dixie thought it would be a laugh to hose him down with water. Unfortunately, he didn't realise it was his clobber Paddy was wearing until it was too late. The rest of the boys rolled about in stitches and Dixie joined in when it dawned on him. I loved moments like that. They relieved the pressure after a game and put you in a relaxed mood for the weekend.

Players must learn to live with pressure, especially playing for the Old Firm, because they are always in the limelight. That was certainly the case the following season, on 17 March 1973, when Celtic played Aberdeen in a Scottish Cup tie which we won 1-0. I was sent off for allegedly kicking Dons full-back Jim Hermiston. It will come as no surprise to Celtic supporters that the referee was a certain Bobby Davidson! I was livid with the decision and a month later faced the SFA beaks at Park Gardens. I defended myself and was cleared of any blame by the disciplinary body. One in the eye for Mr Davidson! In between times I scored twice against Dundee to put Celtic in the Scottish Cup final against Rangers, a match we lost 3-2.

Our eighth league title in succession was then clinched at Easter Road against Hibs. The season once again ended on a high when Celtic defeated Leeds 4-3 at Elland Road in a testimonial match for Jack Charlton which was, and still is, a bit special to me. I could do no wrong and bagged two goals, the second one a long-range shot which had the fans raving. Big Jack said afterwards that my second goal will always be one of his greatest memories. A nice touch from a man with a World Cup winner's medal tucked away in his collection!

Celtic's success story continued in season 1973/74 when we won league title number nine on the trot at Falkirk and lifted the Scottish Cup, defeating Dundee United 3-0 in the final. But for me that season will always be remembered for what happened off the pitch rather than on it.

Chapter Eight

THE DEATH THREAT

Football is supposed to be only a game but try telling that to the butchers of Atletico Madrid. To them it seemed more like a matter of life and death.

Death was certainly on my mind when I endured the most terrifying ordeal of my life on 25 April 1974. Two weeks before, Atletico Madrid had come to Parkhead for the first leg of a European Cup semi-final. Anyone who was at the game will never forget the sheer thuggery of the men from Madrid who masqueraded as footballers. It was like Racing Club all over again.

Ironically, Atletico had a host of Argentinians in their line-up and one of them, Diaz, was well known to Celtic because he had played for Racing Club against us in the World Club Championship. Within minutes of the kick-off he had shown his intentions with a waist-high tackle on me. The game never rose out of the gutter and by the end the Spaniards had three men sent off — Diaz, Quique and Ayala — and seven booked by Turkish referee Mr Babacan. But the animals of Atletico had achieved their aim, to kick us off the park and record a 0-0 draw.

God only knows how the Celtic players and 60,000 fans kept their cool that night. The provocation was unbelievable. And it didn't stop at the final whistle. In the tunnel on the way to the dressing-rooms, I was kicked in the stomach by a Madrid moron who got away unpunished.

For days after the game Celtic waited for UEFA to act and throw Atletico out of the competition to allow us a walkover into the final, but nothing happened. Why they allowed the second game to go ahead I will never know. UEFA's lily-livered approach certainly put lives at risk in Madrid and none more so than mine and big Jock's.

When we arrived on Spanish soil the hostility was on a par with Argentina seven years previously but, unknown to us, the Spanish Press were mainly responsible. They had manufactured a bitter hate campaign against Celtic. They even churned up an age-old war between Spain and Turkey to prove that the referee from the first leg was biased. And they concocted stories which claimed Atletico players had been beaten up by Glasgow policemen. This saddened me because when the Lisbon Lions played in di Stefano's testimonial the Spanish media were unstinting in their praise of Celtic. This time they had maliciously turned fact into fiction and made us look like the villains of the piece at Parkhead.

Armed guards and police escorts followed us everywhere during our three-day stay in the Spanish capital. Even training sessions were conducted with a posse of uniformed officers forming a cordon around the pitch. It was, quite literally, a war zone. Hordes of flag-waving Spaniards followed us back to our hotel on the outskirts of the city, tooting their horns and shouting abuse (thank goodness I didn't understand a word of Spanish).

But the worst moment of my life came on the night before the match. I was rooming, as usual, with Bobby Lennox when the telephone rang about 2 a.m. Bobby awoke first and picked up the receiver before handing it to me. Still half asleep, I answered only to be greeted by a sinister Spanish voice which snarled in broken English "JOHNSTONE, YOU ARE DEAD". Needless to say I had difficulty catching 40 winks that night.

The following morning rumours spread that a sniper was planning to shoot me at the stadium. I was petrified. After breakfast Jock pulled me to one side and revealed that he had also received a threat to his life. So we were both in the firing line. This certainly wasn't what I had bargained for.

I will never forgot Jock's next few lines. Obviously aware that my trousers were in danger of changing colour rapidly he quipped: "Don't worry, wee man. You will be OK. When you start to jink and jive out there nobody will be able to hit you. What about me? I've got to sit in the dugout like a bloody sitting duck."

Despite his calm exterior Jock was taking the threats seriously. Anything was possible in such a volatile city. The Big Man graciously offered me the chance to pull out of the team but I declined. I was as safe on the park as anywhere, I reckoned. But, to

On the move with Celtic.

be honest, the threat worked because I was non-existent during the 90 minutes; although the same could be said for most Celtic players.

The game was just an endurance test. Atletico's dirty tricks were endless. It soon became obvious that their boss, the notorious Argentinian Juan Lorenzo — boss of Lazio when they were banned from European competition a few seasons before for violent conduct — had pulled a fast one at Parkhead. Knowing it was going to be a brawl in Glasgow he left out some of his more skilled players and replaced them with nutters. So the first-leg sending-offs had really not weakened Atletico, with the exception of Ayala who was a danger man when he stopped kicking people.

Two late goals gave Atletico what they were looking for — a place in the European Cup final — but in my opinion the cost was much too high. They had shamed the name of football and should have been banned for a long time. I finished the match with two black eyes but I was glad that my head was still on my shoulders.

The real pity is that Spaniards and Argentinians possess startling skills — you only have to look at Maradona — but too often their win-at-all-costs attitude drags them into the gutter. Atletico certainly got their just desserts that year in the final when Bayern Munich hammered them 4-0 in a replay. But the Spaniards were only a minute away from winning the Cup first time around and that would have been the crime of the century.

I remember Billy Bremner, who was with the Scotland squad somewhere in Europe at the time, telling me later that all the boys watched the replay on TV and most of them cheered as Bayern did the business. But I can't say I did the same. Although we came back from Spain and won the League title for the ninth time in a row with a 1-1 draw at Brockville three days later, I was drained when the final came around. That night in Madrid was the biggest let-down of my life. It had robbed us of the chance to play in a European Cup final for the third time. And after what had happened against Feyenoord I wanted that more than anything else in life.

One of my 23 appearances for Scotland — don't I look overjoyed!

Chapter Nine

TROUBLED WATERS

I played only 23 times for Scotland, a paltry figure compared to Kenny Dalglish, the country's most capped player who has passed the century mark. But during a relatively short period of "national service" I grabbed more controversial headlines than most. I'm not boasting about that but it's true.

Critics often questioned my desire to play for Scotland and to an extent they were right to do so. My reluctance to wear a dark blue shirt can, to a great degree, be traced back to the days when Celtic players, and myself in particular, came in for heavy abuse from the Hampden fans (but more about that later).

Looking back, I can honestly say my small tally of caps doesn't bother me. My first love was Celtic. They paid my wages and I was lucky to play in an era when my club was a top name in European soccer so there was no shortage of glamour ties in which I could show my ability to the world. International duty was a bonus. When it was good it was good but when it was bad — well to borrow a phrase from John McEnroe — it was the pits.

Without doubt the most controversial year of my Scotland career was 1974 when, once again, the demon drink brought about my downfall and robbed me of the chance to play in the final stages of a World Cup. It all started with the infamous Largs rowing boat incident, a melodrama which rocked Scottish football and about which I am still quizzed to this day. Not for the first time I got my name splashed all over the front page of newspapers, a real-life farce which quickly turned into black comedy.

Doing my "national service".

For what it's worth here is my account of the bizarre occasion when a ton of oil was poured, almost literally, on troubled waters! The Home International Championships were being played in the space of a week and all our games were scheduled for Hampden Park. It was a crucial period for Scotland with the World Cup finals in West Germany only weeks away. We were the only home nation to have qualified for the globe's greatest football extravaganza and England — nursing the embarrassment of missing out to Poland — were desperate to give us a sad send-off.

I was left out of the team which went down 1-0 to Northern Ireland on Saturday, 11 May, but I was recalled for the Tuesday night tussle with Wales which we won 2-0, a result which set up a championship decider with England on the following Saturday.

The boys were in buoyant mood on the coach trip back to our base in Largs. We had taken a fair bit of stick from the Press after the defeat by the Irish but our performance against Wales was the perfect response to our critics.

Team boss Willie Ormond gave us the rest of the night off to unwind so when we reached our HQ, the Queens Hotel, the lads headed for a smaller hotel, owned by a guy called Ross Bowie. That way we could relax away from most of the general public. Virtually the whole squad tagged along and we had a great night. Denis Law and captain Billy Bremner, as ever, held court and regaled us with amusing tales from past internationals and English football.

Before I knew it the clock was striking 4 a.m. and most of the boys were merry. I was guttered as we staggered out into the night air. The drink had gone down a treat after the pressures of the game and a lot of the lads were in a party mood.

Big David Harvey, the Leeds United goalkeeper, thought he would have some fun as we walked back to our hotel so he jumped up on to the roof of a small hut near the beach and started pelting the rest of us with stones. Everyone scarpered in different directions. Rangers full-back Sandy Jardine and I ran along the beach to escape the stoning. Within seconds we came upon a stack of rowing boats, all neatly docked on the shingle beach. In my drunken stupor I looked at Sandy and mumbled: "Fancy a wee trip on the water?" "Nae bother," came the reply. So captain courageous Johnstone jumped into a boat and grabbed the oars. I sat, patiently waiting for my buddy to join me. Eventually I shouted: "Sandy are you in yet?" Before I knew it I was out to sea. Sandy had given the boat a hefty kick before collapsing on the beach in stitches! Now I'm no oarsman but I was too drunk to care as the small craft drifted out into deeper water. By the time the rest of the boys arrived to find out what was happening there was no stopping this steaming sailor as I stood up in the boat and gave the whole of Largs a rendering of Rod Stewart's classic *Sailing*. I was just a speck on the dark horizon and that's when the rest of our motley crew started to worry. The joke was over for them but I was oblivious to the dangers.

My old pal Davie Hay and the late Eric Schaedler tried to launch a rescue mission but in true *Titanic* style their boat sank before they had travelled ten yards. Luckily the coastguard, alerted by a disgruntled Largs resident, arrived just in time to pluck the drookit duo from the cold water.

Willie Ormond was on the scene by then, although most of the players legged it when they saw him coming. When the coastguard lifted me ashore the manager gave me a good dressing-down before returning to his bed.

Denis Law was the only player waiting for me on the beach when I arrived looking like a drowned rat. He wrapped a blanket around me and led me back to the hotel where he flung a hot whisky down my neck. Although I was still well "canned" I recall saying to Denis: "The Press will have a field day with this." No doubt fighting back a smile, the Lawman, who was a great wind-up merchant, retorted: "Don't be daft, Jimmy. It will probably only make a few pars in the stop press."

How I wish he had been right. All hell had broken loose and I was front-page news in every paper.

When I staggered down to breakfast later that morning the boys greeted me with an impromptu chorus of *What shall we do with the drunken sailor?*

The media men were on my back straight away. There were calls for me to be axed from the squad and Willie Ormond took a fair bit of stick for his handling of the affair. Depite all the hassle, Willie stuck by me and I will always respect him for that. He could easily have bowed to Press pressure and dropped me like a hot potato but he stuck to his guns — a brave decision in the circumstances. He named me in the team to face England, which lifted me no end. I will never forget that day. We trounced the "Auld Enemy" 2-0 in front of 100,000 Hampden fans who gave me a tremendous reception. We were British champions with the World Cup still to come. I thought all my troubles were behind me . . . how wrong I was.

Ten days later we headed for warm-up games in Belgium and Norway and I was out of the frying pan into the fire. The problems

Putting my right foot forward for Scotland with my pal Bobby Lennox.

started after a 2-1 defeat by the Belgians and again alcohol was the root of all evil. On the flight to Oslo the aircrew dished out free champagne and two individuals in particular were like little boys in a chocolate factory — Billy Bremner and yours truly! We hammered into the free booze along with certain members of the Press corps and by the time we reached our base in Oslo wee Billy and I were "rolling" and oblivious to the scowls on certain SFA officials' faces.

At this point I must briefly mention our accommodation in Oslo. It was literally a student hostel, a high rise block of flats with dormitories. I'm not making excuses for my future actions but the players were cramped together in one small area and the walls were paper thin.

As usual, Billy and I sniffed out the bar before anyone else and parked ourselves down for a quiet drink (you'd think we would have known better). By the time other players wandered in we were well tore. And when the others drifted off to bed we stayed, engaging in a friendly running battle with a clutter of media men. Eventually, in the early hours of the morning, Doc Fitzsimmons — who doubled as the Celtic doctor — persuaded us to return to our rooms. Unfortunately, in our inebriated state, on the way we decided to tell Mr Ormond, who was tucked up in bed, how he should be running his team. That was the final straw. Unknown to us, some SFA officials were in adjoining rooms to Willie and they heard every word of our tirade through the thin walls. They came out straight away and threatened us with all kinds of disciplinary action.

Now Billy and I are both red-haired and quick-tempered. Through our alcoholic haze we decided that enough was enough. So we sauntered off to our rooms muttering: "You can't speak to us like that. We're going home."

The drunken duo packed their bags and togged themselves up in official blazer, trousers and tie and sat waiting for a taxi to take them to the airport. Of course it never arrived. Hours later we awoke — still kitted out in our best clobber — to await the inevitable repercussions of a night on the sauce.

Almost immediately there were cries to send Billy and I home in disgrace but again Ormond refused to bow to outside pressure. He certainly put us in our place but, rather than cause a further stir on the eve of the World Cup, the manager then closed ranks and kept the trouble within the official party. To this day I believe Willie was right. Billy Bremner was Scotland captain and both of us were valuable members of the party. To send us home would have affected the morale of the squad.

I was relieved. To be honest the prospect of flying home early to an inquisition from the Scottish Press did not appeal.

It's history now that Billy skippered Scotland in the games

against Zaire, Brazil and Yugoslavia and played superbly as we came agonisingly close to qualifying for the later rounds. With just a little bit of luck the boys could have pulled off a stunning victory over Brazil.

We came home unbeaten but I paid a terrible price for stepping out of line once too often. Throughout all three games I was forced to sit on the bench without tasting World Cup action. It was Willie's way of punishing me and I can't argue with it. Largs, Belgium and Oslo were just too much for the man to take.

Willie's death was certainly a sad loss to Scottish football. He was one of the fairest men I have met in the game and I will always be grateful for his loyalty.

It was a huge personal blow to miss out on the World Cup but in many ways it was par for the course in my Scotland days which started so well when I won my first cap on my 20th birthday against Wales in Cardiff back in 1965.

In those early days I had a massive inferiority complex and every time I joined up with a Scotland party it seemed to shine through. I suppose I was just in awe of greats like Jim Baxter, Denis Law and Billy Bremner. They were giants of the game and the way they handled themselves in company made me despair. They always looked so composed with the fans or eating in big fancy restaurants. I was still the little boy lost.

My first setback came when I missed the famous "Wembley Wizards" game against England in May 1967, through an injury I picked up playing for Celtic against Dukla Prague in the European Cup semi-final.

I felt even more down in the dumps after our famous win against the World Cup winners. But the incident which really sickened me and led, I suppose, to my disillusionment about playing for Scotland came later that year, in November. I was playing some of the best football of my career at club level but on the international front I still didn't feel at home. *And the boo boys at Hampden didn't help.*

Around that time my great pal, Willie Henderson of Rangers, and I were vying for the right-wing position in the national team. Willie was a great favourite with the fans, especially those at the traditional Rangers end of Hampden. In those days these so-called fans seemed to hate the sight of a Celtic player in Scottish colours. They constantly gave us stick.

That November night, while we were defeating Wales 3-2, it reached an all-time low when I had to endure chants of "Henderson, Henderson" throughout the game. I was devastated.

Scotland boss Bobby Brown delivers a message!

How could fans do this to a player? The barracking had a huge effect on me. I found myself hiding during subsequent matches or giving the ball away quickly — something which was alien to my style of play.

After the Welsh match I became an even bigger fan of Denis Law (if that was possible). Feeling down in the dumps, I was sitting alone during the post-match banquet in Glasgow's Central Hotel when Denis came up and slapped me on the back. "Well done wee man, you were brilliant," he said. I knew otherwise but I will always be grateful to Denis for that gesture. I could have crawled into a hole and no one would have noticed that night but Denis tried to buck me up. It was a terrific tonic from Scotland's greatest-ever striker. A real star on and off the park.

I'm glad to say times have changed and Scotland fans are much more tolerant nowadays. It's more like a club atmosphere on the terracings. But in those days the boo boys did me no favours and that still sticks in my throat.

The following year another incident occurred which had my critics and the rumour-mongers rubbing their hands with glee. It was February and Scotland were due to face England in a vital European Nations Cup qualifying tie. Games against the Sassenachs always generate fierce passion but this one had an additional edge. England only needed a draw to qualify for the latter stages of the Cup. A win would see us through.

There was a lot of speculation over whether I would be in the line-up but when boss Bobby Brown named his team I was left out in the cold. The front four were to be Charlie Cooke of Chelsea, Bobby Lennox, Alan Gilzean of Spurs and Willie Johnston.

Bobby Brown said I wasn't mentally prepared and it was fair comment because I was having troubles at Celtic. But the Press went to town again. They had implied all along that Mr Brown and I didn't see eye to eye which simply wasn't true. I got on well with the man and I know he rated me as a player. The guy I had no time for was his assistant, Walter McCrae, who promoted the biggest row before the Nations Cup-tie.

Scotland had arranged a private practice match in Largs with Celtic and that morning McCrae approached me and said: "I want you to run the line for me in this match." I thought he was joking. Me, act as a linesman against my clubmates. Talk about degrading. I would have been a laughing stock. I told McCrae, in no uncertain terms, to "get lost".

The story leaked out although the Press got hold of the wrong end of the stick. They thought the row had been with Mr Brown and that fuelled speculation that we hated each other's guts.

Ironically, Alan Gilzean was injured in the practice match and the boss asked me to play against England. But my mind was in a turmoil and I declined. Big John Hughes took my place but England managed a 1-1 draw which saw them through. I watched and wondered whether I had done the right thing.

It was a very black time in my football life. The only bright spot came shortly after that Hampden game when Celtic whipped Kilmarnock 6-0 at Rugby Park. Walter McCrae was boss of Killie and I played a blinder. As I came off the park I shouted to McCrae: "Not bad for a linesman, Walter." He ignored me but I'm sure he was fuming inside.

An even bigger storm broke in May 1969, before another game against England, this time at Wembley. And again I was at the centre of the controversy. My main critic this time was Jock Stein and once more the media assumed I was deliberately shunning Scotland. I had been suspended in April for accumulating three bookings, which cost me a place in Celtic's Cup final team against Rangers. I also missed home internationals against Wales and Northern Ireland. Bobby Brown called me into the squad for the England game but because of the suspension I didn't feel in the right shape to face the Sassenachs. I asked Stein for advice and he said that if I didn't want to be considered I should make this clear to Bobby Brown personally, which I did on the night of the Ireland match at Hampden. But Bobby was still very keen to include me in his plans so I changed my mind and reported with the rest of the squad to the North British Hotel in Glasgow. Unfortunately, that night I began to feel very off colour. My temperature rose rapidly. I knew there was something wrong but the team doctor just gave me a few pills.

The following morning Jock answered an SOS call from Scotland officials to bring my boots to the hotel. The Big Man was obviously confused but I didn't get a chance to explain my change of mind when he arrived at the hotel.

Later the rest of the Scotland squad set off for London by air. Eddie McCreadie and I were given permission to travel by train because we both disliked flying. We boarded a train from Glasgow to Edinburgh where we would catch a connection to London. But on the journey to Edinburgh I was physically sick. There was no way I could travel to London so when we reached Waverley Station I rang Abbotsinch Airport and, fortunately, caught Bobby Brown. I explained my problems and he instructed me to go straight home to bed. But no sooner had I arrived in Lanarkshire

Taking on the Auld Enemy.

when the telephone rang. It was Jock, asking me to visit Celtic Park straight away. When I arrived he gave me the biggest roasting of my life. Jock was furious that I had changed my mind without telling him. He disliked the idea of having to act as a message boy with my boots but my ultimate withdrawal from the squad, well that broke the camel's back. He called me for everything and would not listen to my side of the story. Later he released a statement to the Press which read: "Bobby Brown obviously needs players he can depend upon and Jimmy Johnstone is not in that category. It seems to me that Mr Brown would be well advised to go ahead without him in future."

The newspapers lapped it up. Here was me pulling out of an England game for the third time. Some suggested it was the end of my international career.

What really annoyed me about the whole affair was that I was genuinely ill. A medical certificate from the doctor who examined me at home proved I had tonsilitis and a temperature of 100 degrees.

Needless to say, I felt worse when I dragged myself to the TV on the Saturday to witness a 4-1 thrashing for Scotland.

In October of that year I was sensationally recalled to the national squad and scored a goal in an unlucky 3-2 defeat by West Germany in a World Cup qualifying tie.

But certainly my best game for Scotland came two years later, on 11 November 1971, against Belgium at Pittodrie. We won 1-0 and I laid on the goal for John O'Hare. The sheer relief of playing away from Hampden Park inspired me that night. I really turned on the style. The Aberdeen fans were extraordinary and chanted my name constantly. There wasn't a boo boy in sight. I always thought they should have played more Scotland games in the Granite City!

Tommy Docherty had been appointed temporary manager of Scotland a few months earlier and it seemed like the dawning of a new era.

Talk of the 'Doc' brings me around again to another drink-related incident which backfired badly. One night leading up to an international myself and George Graham, now manager of Arsenal, sneaked into Tommy's room and pinched two bottles of champers. Don't ask me why but we certainly enjoyed the stolen goods. Of course the Doc blew his top when he found out what had happened and told me I would never play for my country again. I would like to point out that I replaced the champagne at a later date but I suppose that's where I came in . . . talking about drink and the curse it put on my career.

Chapter Ten

BIGOTRY AND THE BLUES

The Old Firm clash between Celtic and Rangers is often hailed as the greatest club match on earth, and rightly so. There's not an atmosphere like it when the Glasgow giants clash at Parkhead, Ibrox or Hampden.

Quite simply, it's a game all on its own. The result means everything to both clubs and their supporters . . . often for reasons far removed from football. Previous form counts for nothing and potential matchwinners can freeze on the day because of the pressure.

I can't honestly say I enjoyed playing against Rangers. The tension was unbearable and often victory was more of a relief than a reward. For me the pressure started days before a ball was kicked. Fans would stop me in the street and virtually demand a win. It was life or death stuff. I hardly slept the night before an Old Firm meeting. Everything would go through my head and often I would break into a cold sweat just thinking of what lay in store. I'm sure I kicked every ball and scored every goal 24 hours in advance.

Of course we were heroes come 4.40 p.m. on a Saturday if Rangers had been beaten. Overjoyed fans would phone me at home, strangers would pat me on the back and even women would offer generous votes of thanks. Defeat, though, was unthinkable. It meant weeks, maybe months, in the doghouse.

Of course, most of the pressure surrounding Celtic v Rangers games stems from the religious bigotry which exists in Scotland. Catholics and Protestants can work side by side during the week but when an Old Firm game comes around they go to separate ends of the park. There would be nothing wrong with this if it was just plain, good old-fashioned rivalry but a small minority on each side of the fence stirs up hatred on the terracing which produces a powder-keg atmosphere.

Thankfully, the hatred doesn't spill over on to the park too often (at least not in my day). Sure, there would be wind-ups, players calling each other "Orange so and so's" or a "Fenian without a father" but it was heat of the moment stuff. I certainly held no grudge against Rangers players in general.

Can the bigotry be stopped? It's a touchy subject, much like "Will Rangers ever sign a Catholic?" I hope the bigotry ends but I must be honest and say that I can't see it happening in my day. It's too deep-rooted. Rangers' openly admitted sectarian policy from the past, which bars players of the Catholic faith playing for them, has kept the pressure pot boiling. So have the troubles in Northern Ireland. That's evident from the "political" chants heard at Parkhead and Ibrox.

In my view the present Rangers chiefs are handling the "Catholic question" quite well. I believe men like chairman David Holmes and manager Graeme Souness want to rectify what they see as a serious situation. But, on the other side of the coin, it would be very difficult for a Catholic to sign for Rangers. Can you imagine me, red hair and all, turning out for them in my heydey! The "stick" from the stands would have been severe. Seriously, any RC is bound to take major abuse from a percentage of the Ibrox faithful. Some supporters would probably turn their backs on the club if they made such a momentous move — although I doubt if Souness would lose much sleep over them.

Talking of Souness, I've got to admire Rangers for appointing him as manager at Ibrox. They wanted back to the top so they got a top man. Graeme's knowledge of the game is vast. He learned his trade at Liverpool and there can be few better "apprenticeships" than that. Playing in Italy has also given him a chance to build up foreign contacts which could be invaluable to the 'Gers. Already, he has put Scottish football firmly on the world map by signing top stars like Terry Butcher, Graham Roberts, Chris Woods and Mark Walters from England. Everybody is talking about what's happening north of the border and that can only be good for our game. Even the English Press have woken up to the fact that our national sport is not caber-tossing after all!

Souness is an uncompromising character — both on and off the park — and inevitably he has already been involved in his fair share of Old Firm controversy, after being sent off at Parkhead last season. But then I'm no stranger to that scene. I got my marching orders, whisper it, for the sixth time in my career back on 25 August 1973, at Parkhead, following an incident with Alex MacDonald. In the heat of the battle I grabbed "Doddy" and a scuffle ensued. To this day I claim Alex feigned injury as he fell to the ground but referee "Tiny" Wharton thought otherwise and sent me packing. I was fined £150 and suspended for 14 days.

"Doddy" was one Rangers player I certainly didn't like on the park. I always felt he went out to rile Celtic players. He was a bit nasty and made a lot of enemies for going in late on tackles. Professional players hate that. It's a dangerous tactic which can lead to serious injury and subsequent loss of earnings. It must be built into Alex because he did it to me a few years ago in a charity game at Ibrox and I wasn't amused. Maybe Old Firm rivalry never dies!

Eric Caldow was another Ranger I didn't relish meeting — but for a different reason. Eric was a good player, very quick and clever with it and I seldom got much change out of this fine full-back.

But I suppose John Greig is the Rangers player I have most cause to remember. Greigy and I had dozens of highly charged duels and I've still got the bruises to prove it! John was surely one of Rangers' most loyal servants. He captained them through the lean years when Celtic had a stranglehold on the league title. We gave Rangers the occasional crumb of comfort in Cup competitions but it must have been an agonising time for "scrambled egg" — my nickname for John — and his mates. Throughout his career Greigy was a fierce but fair competitor. I wouldn't class him as dirty although maybe in the heat of the battle I thought otherwise.

I recall one New Year's Day game back in the 1970s when I gave the former Rangers captain and manager a torrid time. Conditions were atrocious underfoot after heavy rain. It was the sort of day big defenders dread and Greigy wasn't enjoying it one little bit. Three times I "skinned" him on the wing and on each occasion he fouled me as I tried to pass. The third time I was lying on the deck injured when referee Bobby Davidson — there's that name cropping up again — ran up and told me to stop clowning around and get on with the game. I was astonished but then Bobby and I rarely saw eye to eye.

But there were no bad feelings between Greigy and I. Both of us had a job to do and there was no quarter asked or given. To this day I think John holds the unofficial record for keeping me up with his boot while I was in the air after a tackle. Most defenders got two touches but Greigy often managed three! We are still good buddies. A few years ago I was at Ibrox for an Old Firm game when John was Rangers' manager. As ever, it was a tense occasion but when John spied me coming in the main door he strolled up with open arms and stood laughing and joking for ten minutes. I will always appreciate the gesture because John must have been under pressure at the time.

My other two great Ibrox pals were Willie Henderson and Jim Baxter. What a pair of characters. Willie was a real mate of mine despite our rivalry for club and country. Both of us fought for the right-winger's jersey in the Scotland team for years but it didn't affect our friendship off the park. Willie had all the individual skills of a world-class performer and a sense of humour to match. I remember one Old Firm tussle when Tommy Gemmell was giving him a hard time. After one foul the wee man crashed to the ground but was up in a flash, waving a finger in Tam's face. The fans were at fever pitch. They expected a barney but of course didn't realise what Willie was saying. As they faced each other only inches apart Willie quipped: "Any more of that, big man, and we're not going for a pint after the game!" If only the fans had known. Maybe it would have taken the heat out of the occasion.

"Slim" Jim must be one of Scotland's all-time greats. The man was a magician with the ball. He teased and tormented even top-class opposition. Jim was blessed with genius and he never tired of putting on a show. His special skills gave him the chance to be arrogant on the park and the fans lapped it up. Baxter was quite amazing. He never felt pressure on big occasions.

I must recount a story I heard about Jim and wee Willie before an international at Hampden. A television reporter was quizzing "Slim" about how he handled the tension of playing for his country. Jim was warming up on the park with Henderson at the time and when the pushy media man pressed for an answer Jim turned to him and said in a broad Fife accent: "Pressure. Oh, aye, it can shatter you. Sometimes it's very hard to cope with." The reporter rushed off with his "scoop" but, unknown to him, "Slim" and Willie were the calmest men in the stadium. During the warm-up they had been having bets on who could hit the crossbar most times — at £20 a shot!

But even Jim and Willie couldn't predict the outcome of Old Firm games. As I've said, the form book could be thrown out the window when the big two got together. There was no finer example of this than the 1966 Scottish Cup final in which Rangers defeated

Celtic 1-0 after a replay, thanks to a Kai Johansen goal. Celtic were on the way to the league title and three months earlier had reached the semi-finals of the European Cup Winners Cup only to lose out to Liverpool 2-1 on aggregate. Rangers were in complete disarray at the time. They were plagued by injuries and sent out a team with forwards playing in defence and half-backs up front. We completely roasted the Ibrox men and had about 95 per cent of the pressure. Balls were kicked off the Rangers line regularly as they rode their luck. Then, with one kick of the ball from Kai, the Cup was won. We couldn't believe it but it was a timely reminder that nothing can be taken for granted when the Old Firm go to war.

The tables turned at the end of the following season as Celtic clinched the title for the second time in a row with a 2-2 draw against our south side rivals only two weeks before we set off for Lisbon. The game is still one of my favourite Old Firm memories because I scored both Celtic goals. The second is still vivid in my mind today. On a really heavy pitch, I cut inside beating a few Rangers players in the process. I ran for what seemed like an eternity before firing a rocket shot with my bad foot — the left peg — into the net. I couldn't believe my luck. The rest of the boys were ecstatic as they jumped all over me but I couldn't share their feelings. I was just bloody exhausted after my long run and tried to shove them off.

My other unforgettable memory against Rangers came on 12 May 1971, when we defeated them 2-1 in a Scottish Cup final replay at Hampden. Incidentally, I played at inside-right that night although if I'd been named at full-back it would scarcely have mattered. It was just one of those nights when everything I touched turned to gold and I was hailed as the star of the show. Bobby Charlton was in the crowd and it gave me deep personal satisfaction to turn on the style in front of such a legendary figure.

Victory that night made up for the misery of two years previously when I was forced to sit on the sidelines through suspension as Celtic hammered Rangers 4-0 in the Scottish Cup final, a game which was controlled by George Connelly, an extraordinary talent who unfortunately drifted out of football long before his time.

Sadly, 1971 will be remembered by everyone in Scotland for the tragic Ibrox Disaster in which 66 people died on 2 January at the end of an Old Firm game. The game itself was heading for a goalless draw when Bertie Auld fired a ball through the thick mist and I popped up in the outside-left position to head home. With only a minute to go Celtic seemed home and dry and Rangers fans

Keeping the heid with a perfect penalty against Rangers in a Drybrough Cup shoot out.

started to drift off. But they came running back seconds later when Colin Stein grabbed a last-gasp equaliser. In the resultant crush on Stairway 13 the death toll reached 66.

I knew nothing about the scale of the disaster until well after the game when the Celtic players were on the club coach outside

Ibrox. We were growing impatient waiting for the directors who, we presumed, were still sampling the free hospitality in the Ibrox boardroom. But then John Fitzsimmons, our team doctor, rushed on board and told us the news. By this time ambulances were flying everywhere but we were told to stay on the bus — there was nothing we could do. Like all the players, I was stunned. My thoughts were with the relatives whose sons and fathers were fated never to return from the game. The result of a football game, even one as big as an Old Firm clash, meant nothing in the light of such a tragedy. It was a day when pointless bigotries were forgotten and everyone connected with Celtic and Rangers was united in grief.

Ironically, I hated playing at Ibrox, a feeling shared by most Celtic players. I'm sure Rangers lads would say the same about Parkhead. I was rarely confident of getting a result in their backyard. The abuse from Rangers' fans didn't bother me. It was just part and parcel of the most passionate club match in the world. I'm glad to say in recent years I've had a warm welcome at various Rangers Supporters Clubs. No, I've not changed my allegiance but it's nice to know that, to most Old Firm fans, football still means more than bigotry.

Chapter Eleven

MY BLACKEST DAY

Picking up my P45 from Parkhead is the hardest thing I've ever done. And even now, all those years later, I have difficulty talking about the day when I collected my boots and walked out the doors at Celtic Park for the last time as a player. After the happiest 14 years of my life the party was over. I had been given my "books". I couldn't bear to take a last look back. I felt like a prisoner being sent to Death Row with no leave of appeal and next to no chance of a reprieve. It was an all-time low in my life, a nightmare which still comes back to haunt me.

The trouble was I couldn't imagine life after Celtic. Parkhead had been the focal point of my world since I walked in the door and I thought it would remain that way forever. Not once in my long love affair with the club did I stop to think when it might end. So I was prepared in no way for the dreaded news which came like a bolt out of the blue on 10 June 1975.

In some ways it was the end of a sad season for Celtic as their long stranglehold on the Scottish league title had been broken for the first time in nearly a decade by our arch-rivals, Rangers, who won the title with 56 points. We were well adrift in third place on 45 points, three behind Hibs. And despite doing a Cup double — the Scottish Cup and League Cup both came to Parkhead that season — it wasn't enough for Celtic or their fans. We had defeated Airdrie in the final of the "Scottish" and overcame Hibs 6-3 in a thrilling League Cup final. But Celtic treated the title like their own private property and losing it was a crushing blow to our prestige. Towards the tail end of the season I wasn't a first team regular but, at 30, I still felt fit and well and was looking forward to a summer break in which to recharge my batteries for fresh challenges ahead.

A month previously Billy McNeill had hung up his boots after the Scottish Cup final win, leaving only two Lisbon Lions at Parkhead, myself and Bobby Lennox. But it didn't cross my mind that something was amiss when Jock Stein said the board of directors wanted to see me. I had been up in front of them before on a few occasions, so I didn't give it a second thought. But when Chairman Desmond White broke the news that Celtic were giving me a free transfer I was speechless. Tears welled up in my eyes as I virtually keeled over with shock. The club's offer of a joint testimonial match with Bobby Lennox the following season completely passed over me as I was consoled and led out a side door. Director Jimmy Farrell drove me home, but the journey was just a blur. I was still in a daze as Jimmy broke the news to my wife Agnes, who was naturally very upset. My kids were too young to realise that their dad was out of work.

But playing for Celtic was much more than a job to me. It was a pleasure and an honour and I could not fathom what to do without it. Going back to Parkhead a few days later was a horrible ordeal. The rest of the players were already on holiday, so the silence was deafening. I could hardly utter a word to anyone as I picked up my bits and pieces. I was completely choked.

Celtic gave me very little by way of an explanation for their decision although I presume it was just another step in building for the future.

For days I lay around in a deep depression but bills had to be paid and I had a wife and three young children to provide for. Football was my only skill, I had no other trade, which is a problem most players face at some time.

The first offer for my services came a few days later from New York Cosmos. Football was just taking off in the United States and Cosmos offered me a considerable sum to play in their eight-week season. But I wanted the security of a three-year deal so I knocked them back. A week later they signed the incomparable Pele, my all-time hero. But, in hindsight, I have no regrets about turning my back on the "Big Apple" and the possible chance to play alongside the priceless Brazilian. I had visited New York before and found it pretty horrific. Anything could happen there, and often did. I reckoned it was not the place for my family to live.

By this time representatives of San Jose Earthquake had approached me, asking if I would like to come to California. I

Getting down to it in San Jose.

fancied the sound of the "Sunshine State" and quickly negotiated highly lucrative terms for the eight-week season over the telephone. I flew out from Heathrow Airport three or four days before my wife and kids but, as ever, trouble followed me. On arrival in Canada, en route to California, I was grilled by an officious customs man and told to report to immigration staff. At that time there was a lot of resentment among Canadians to footballers. They strongly objected to the fact that players could walk into their country without a work permit, make a quick killing, and leave. I was worried in case they might find some technical reason to put me on the first plane home so I telephoned

99

the commercial manager of San Jose who sorted the situation out and I continued my journey after receiving a severe lecture on the ethics of my business from an irate immigration woman. Nowadays players need work permits to play across the Atlantic, so I suppose the Canadians are happier.

Unfortunately, I arrived in California with only the clothes I was wearing. Talk about accident-prone! My luggage had been sent on the connecting flight I missed due to the delay at customs and it took me three days to recover it.

My reception committee in California was astonishing. Every media man in the State seemed to be there. Pele couldn't have caused a bigger stir. Everyone wanted pictures and I was happy to oblige. A car salesman even offered me a Rolls Royce and that sparked off one of the most hilarious episodes of my life. The salesman was a real wide boy — the type who could sell sun tan oil to an Eskimo. The Roller was a vintage which had seen better days. The American Arthur Daley told me I could have use of it for playing along with his publicity stunt and I agreed to pick it up in about a week's time. There was no way I was getting into a car right away. If you've never been to America, let me tell you driving is like dicing with death. Real crazy-horses! I could not get used to driving on the right-hand side of the road. And the traffic lights, well they confused the life out of me! Unlike Britain, they are suspended in the sky and as often as not I had driven through a red light without realising. I crashed three times. It was like a scene from Wacky Races! Fortunately, my little team-mate Johnny Moore, the Scot who contacted me when I left Celtic, drove me around for the first week until it was time to collect the Roller. Or so I thought.

When I arrived at the garage, accompanied by Johnny, the wide boy tried to fob me off with a right old banger. I quickly sussed out the situation and turned to Johnny, saying: "We'll have to forget that TV commercial now." Johnny twigged immediately as the gullible salesman took the bait.

"What commercial?" he replied, quick as a flash.

"Och, it was just something a TV station wanted to do when they heard you were giving me a Roller," I lied.

Within seconds our excited friend had offered me his car, a beautiful Buick with air-conditioning, tinted windows, the lot.

Of course, there was no commercial and I would have been on a winner but for a disastrous piece of driving. I jumped into the Buick only to ram into the old banger which had been offered to me. Johnny couldn't stop laughing as we drove off at high speed

God, how embarrassing! American razzmatazz has just gone too far.

with damaged paintwork from the Buick flying everywhere. Needless to say the shocked salesman retrieved his pride and joy a few days later. But maybe I taught him a lesson.

San Jose was one long party and I loved almost every minute of it . . . well almost. A day after arriving I walked into the bank to open up an account, to be told by the teller that only an hour earlier he had been held up at gunpoint by a raider!

Violence apart, I must hand it to the Yanks. They promoted football to perfection and made it a truly family occasion. Our stadium had a capacity of around 25,000 and was packed for every game. Fans would turn up three hours before kick-off and set up barbecues outside on an acre of grass. After eating hamburgers and drinking Budweiser they piled into the stadium with their kids. This created a happy atmosphere which the players appreciated. But one thing I didn't appreciate was being introduced individually to the crowd. A fanfare would go up and each player would run out, flanked on both sides by pretty cheerleaders, as the announcer called out his name. We were all asked to do a little turn. The centre-half jumped up and headed the ball but I just strolled out. I found it all a little too embarrassing.

The razzmatazz was something else. I remember the most way-out character was a guy, aptly named "Crazy George". He would run along the top of the dugouts battering a big drum to get the fans going. He never missed a game and was always up to something different. One day he hadn't appeared and the players were bemused. It was about ten minutes before kick-off. George was going to ruin his record. Next thing we heard was a helicopter hovering about 1,000 feet up and there was George being lowered into the stadium on a rope ladder, beating his big drum.

On another occasion George tried to rope me into doing a wee stint with a tiger. He wanted me to play "keepy up" in front of the wild animal but I said, "No way." Have you ever seen a real live tiger? Well, I assure you it is a frightening sight.

Throughout my stay I had first-class treatment. Before Agnes and the kids arrived I was put up in a palatial hotel but we moved into a condominium when the family were united. The weather was hot all the time. Grapes and oranges hung from the trees and the kids loved messing around in the swimming pool, although Agnes was a bit homesick. We trained at about 9 p.m. because of the humidity and I enjoyed it immensely. I never missed a session. The Earthquake boys were great fun and what a cosmopolitan lot! We had Mexicans, Poles, Jamaicans, Englishmen, Scots and Yugoslavs.

The Slavs certainly infiltrated the positions of power. The club was owned by a millionaire Yugoslavian and, not surprisingly, the coach and captain were his fellow countrymen. They were murder. If the Slav section didn't want anyone else to know what was going on they rabbited away in their own lingo while the rest of us sat mystified. The annoying thing was they could all speak English! Admittedly, the coach's English wasn't the best but that didn't stop him during tactics talks.

The man's favourite possession was his blackboard. He was heavily influenced by American football, so there was chalk everywhere, but most of it was nonsense. My other little mucker Davie Kemp, a former Junior player from Stirling, Mooro and I found it all a scream but the Americans took it all in.

Most of the Earthquake boys were good company. After training most nights we would go to a pizza parlour together and sit until well after midnight eating and drinking chargers of beer surrounded by lovely little Mexican kids. It was such a relaxed atmosphere. Looking back, I could have become a multi-millionaire during my stay in California. Around that time skateboards came on the market in America for the first time. I tried one out but thought nothing of it. Two years later they took off like a bomb in Britain. If I'd twigged at the time and got a franchise to push them in the UK, who knows what might have happened? I still think about it.

But anyone who knows me will testify that I'm more like Michael Crawford than J R Ewing. That was certainly borne out during an incident in Canada which could have come straight out of a *Carry On* movie. Needless to say, the central character was again yours truly.

Earthquake were in Vancouver during a three-game trip over the border. The coach told us to relax, so the boys went down to the swimming pool in the basement of our hotel. It was closed off to the public so the lads stripped off for a spot of "skinny dipping". Myself and a little Mexican called Manny were new to the squad at the time so the other players thought they would hold an initiation ceremony. They made a dive for us in the water and caught Manny but I escaped and jumped out of the pool and ran towards the lift, with a pack in pursuit. Fortunately, the door was open so I leapt in, managing to keep the vultures at bay. I was off the hook, or so I thought. But my room was on the 16th floor and to my horror the lift stopped for the first time — on the ground floor, slap bang in the middle of a foyer packed with residents. All hell broke loose as

Fellow Quakers, Johnny Moore (left) and Davie Kemp.

shocked women screamed at the sight of a little red-haired man parading around starkers.

My explanation fell on deaf ears, so I frantically but unsuccessfully tried to hide my manhood and press the button at the same time. I was in a panic, thinking about what would happen if the newspapers back home got wind of this. I would have been crucified.

Meanwhile, the lift was climbing again. I stared at the counter and prayed as it rose . . . 10, 11, 12, 13, 14, ding! It had stopped again just one floor from safety. I could hardly bear to look as the door opened and this enormous American woman came into view. Well, she erupted and let out the biggest howl I have ever heard, before running off down the corridor.

I was nearly in tears by the time I reached the 16th floor to discover, of course, I had no key. I wondered what would happen if someone came out of a room. The police would be called and I would be charged with indecent exposure. Then I spied the emergency stairs. It was my only option, so I sat there for over half an hour.

Now, the temperature in Vancouver was well below zero and the stairs were made of concrete so I was frozen when the rest of the boys returned. Obviously they found it all highly amusing but my heart was beating so hard I could hardly speak. It was one of the few times the old "ticker" worked overtime.

I've always enjoyed playing football and the Californian public certainly went wild on the few occasions I turned it on for San Jose. They loved the dribbling and touches of showmanship. My best performance and biggest compliment came when we met New York Cosmos. I played a blinder in the first half and as we lined up after the interval an opponent put his hand out and patted my back before muttering a few highly complimentary words about my ball skills. I felt ten feet tall (and that takes a bit of doing). It is still one of the biggest compliments I've ever received because it came from a man who has no equal . . . Pele.

But I rarely put 100 per cent commitment into games. A bad performance or a defeat didn't affect me like in the days at Parkhead when the boys climbed mountains every week. My heart wasn't in it. It was still back at Celtic Park.

Chapter Twelve

MY BATTLE WITH THE BOOZE

My life really hit the skids after I signed for Sheffield United. Around then I was still in mourning after the heartbreaking split from Celtic. The spell in America eased the pain briefly but a deep depression was hanging over me when out of the blue Jimmy Sirrell, then manager of United, asked me down to Bramall Lane. I was very impressed with the man and the set-up in Sheffield so I signed a two-year contract in November, 1975.

But what should have been a new beginning turned into a battle with the booze. As everyone must know by now, I enjoy a drink but in Yorkshire a pastime became a problem time. Without Celtic, football was pretty meaningless in my eyes so I turned to the bar for consolation. It was a far cry from the Lisbon era. Back in those days I hammered myself in training from Monday to Friday, often volunteering to come back maybe two afternoons a week for more. Most of the Lions did the same. The weekend was the only time we had a "blow-out" and anyone who swallowed a lot of beer on a Saturday night certainly worked it off on a Monday morning with a punishing session.

Celtic fans deserved nothing less. They were our number one priority and we could not bear to let them down. That's how professional and proud Celtic players were back in those glorious years. No Lion ever complained about being overworked. Any sacrifice was worth it for the green and white legions. A lot of people may not believe this but even I toed the line by staying indoors every Friday night and most other nights during ten years at the top with Celtic.

Back then I recall my mates Billy Bremner and Denis Law telling me how the atmosphere was much more relaxed down south. Players could wander down to their local for a few beers without any problem — even on a Friday night. Clubs didn't frown on such an action. This was reiterated by my good friend Bobby Murdoch when he was at Middlesbrough. But I didn't believe it until I arrived in Sheffield and saw the evidence for myself.

My old pals were certainly spot on with their information. Players could enjoy a drink at most times without being carpeted. This was alien to me but I took advantage of the relaxed rules and fell into a dangerous rut.

I began drinking more than ever before — probably every second night I would have a good bucket. It was mostly beer — about six to eight pints — but sometimes I would throw back a few "shorts" as well. And I wasn't alone. Other Sheffield players were also hitting the sauce.

For the first few weeks, before Agnes and the kids arrived, I stayed in the same hotel as Jimmy Sirrell. Often I would ring the receptionist and ask whether Jimmy was in or out. If the answer was "out" then I brought some lads back to the hotel, the Kenwood, for a late-night bevvy session.

I began to treat Sheffield like one long party and the atmosphere at Bramall Lane didn't help. The place was full of mercenaries, players who were just in it for the money. They had no loyalty to the club. Transfers were taking place left, right and centre. There was no passion or "playing for the jersey" spirit, something I could not understand after so many years of devoted service to Celtic. But I fell into the trap of thinking "I'm all right, Jack". I was sitting pretty with a two-year contract. The money was all right — not on the massive scale of Manchester United, Spurs or Liverpool, but enough to make life comfortable. Why not enjoy it? So I became a mercenary.

Almost inevitably, the bevvying increased. I began to miss training sessions and, even if I did turn up, I was often just going through the motions as the effects of the night before wore off.

At one time I was drinking very heavily. Maybe I didn't disgrace myself on the park but I was cheating the Sheffield fans and manager Sirrell.

Sometimes I would go on the wagon for a few days then have a binge. Looking back it was a serious situation, something I wouldn't wish to go through again. *I was going to the dogs.*

Thankfully, I began to get a grip just before it was too late. Gradually I began to realise how much I was hurting my family and

My favourite team . . . At home with the family and grand-daughter Emma.

friends. My personality changed after a good drink and I would be abusive to everyone around me, including my wife and children. Frankly I was becoming a Jekyll and Hyde character.

A drunk isn't the best of company. He keeps anti-social hours and ignores the people who matter most. He is too busy nursing a hangover to care about making other people happy.

I didn't want to end up an alcoholic so I slowly began to cut down my drinking. OK, I was no angel but I began to get my head together. It was a slow process but by now my family were around me in a lovely house in High Green which helped me return to normal.

On the pitch I rarely set the heather on fire but the same could be said for most of the Sheffield players. However, I served out my contract. Now, would Sheffield have allowed this to happen if I had turned into an alcoholic? I think not. I would have been told to get on my bike within weeks.

To this day I'm grateful to my wife Agnes, my children and friends for sticking by me during the rough patches over the years. Agnes, in particular, has been through the mill a few times. I can only say through the pages of this book that I'm sincerely sorry for all the heartache and worry I have caused and that I love them all dearly.

Perhaps because of what I've been through I feel qualified to comment on the part drinking plays in football. Make no mistake, the temptation is there for players to overindulge all the time. It's amazing how many people bend over backwards to please a star name. They pat you on the back and buy a drink almost as a matter of course. Doors into many different worlds open up to boys who may, like myself, come from a humble background, and it's easy to fall by the wayside.

For many players a drink is part and parcel of a Saturday. If their team wins then it's out to celebrate at a pub or club. Defeat often means drowning their sorrows with a few beers.

The bigger the star, the larger the pitfalls of course. Megastars like George Best and Jimmy Greaves have been slated in the past for hitting the bottle. But I admire both men immensely, not for drinking but for holding their hands up and freely admitting the problem. Greavsie is now a reformed alcoholic, a TV personality and something of a national hero and George, while still not a choirboy, is a successful London businessman.

Sometimes I wonder if the general public realise the pressures of living in the fast lane. I'm not condoning drunkenness but I would like to take an ordinary man off the street and put him in the shoes of Bestie, Greavsie or myself for a week at the height of our careers and see if all the fame and fortune would change them or lead them into bad habits. I wouldn't bet against it.

Incidentally, I favour English football's approach when it comes to the thorny question of players having a drink. As long as they stick to the rules, and don't go over the top like I did, a quiet drink — even on a Friday — will do no lasting damage. It would allow players to live a more normal lifestyle.

In Scotland, especially playing for the Old Firm, it's like living in a goldfish bowl. A player would be crucified by a club and the Press if spotted in a pub on a Friday night. The public wouldn't take long to inform the newspapers and a story can be exaggerated from there.

Maybe we are too narrow-minded on the subject of drinking. Footballers are, after all, human beings. Rugby doesn't get the same kind of bad press, which surprises me because it's no secret that a large percentage of rugger boys are famous for the amount of alcohol they can consume. Talking of rugby players I can't resist recounting one of the few amusing stories from Sheffield which I heard from the night porter at the Kenwood hotel. I apologise in advance to all the ladies (I'm not really a male chauvinist pig).

Anyway, this crowd of rugby players were staying at the hotel one night and drinking away when one smart Alex came up with a bright idea. Each player threw a fiver on the table and the bet was who could pull the worst-looking "bird" at the dancing. The winner would collect the handsome kitty which was left for safe keeping with the captain's wife — the only lady in the company — as the tanked-up team sped off to a local disco.

Around 2 a.m. most had filtered back with their respective partners and there were some "beauties" among them. There was just one guy to come and the rest of his team-mates anxiously waited to see where the money was going. All of a sudden the door flew open and this madame, who was no Maria Whittaker or Linda Lusardi, walked in, to an almighty roar. The poor girl didn't know what was going on and she was even more bemused when her gallant escort started leaping up and down like a constipated monkey. Needless to say he had won the bet! Maybe it's not funny to females but I can't help imagining the looks on the girls' faces when they realised the boozey boys had set them up.

Although my roots will always be firmly in Viewpark, I liked living in Yorkshire for a spell. The people of Sheffield were fabulous — right down to earth. I have all the time in the world for them. The atmosphere was so different from Glasgow because there was no bigotry lurking under the surface. But the citizens of the "steel city" had the same sharp sense of humour as Glaswegians.

110

However, Bramall Lane was a different kettle of fish, as I've said. I arrived during the season when the Blades were relegated from Division One. There was a lot of in-fighting between the players and management. Cliques were the order of the day.

Jimmy Sirrell didn't seem too happy at Sheffield and I feel he lost the place a bit after taking the drop into the Second Division. Some players certainly lost respect for him. I remember one guy who was out of favour at the time sleeping through one of Jimmy's tactics talks. It was an insulting gesture, one which I couldn't comprehend after years under Jock Stein. But even in the bad times Jimmy, who was a bit of an eccentric character, could be humorous. I remember one time when we arrived at the training ground in a fleet of cars but the manager was nowhere to be seen. Half an hour later he arrived, in the passenger seat of a friend's car, and duly apologised for being late. Jimmy explained that he had been in an accident and then suddenly pointed at Simon Stainrod, saying: "And it was all your f------ fault." Young Simon, who later moved to Queens Park Rangers, Aston Villa and Stoke City, naturally looked bewildered as Jimmy continued his monologue. "I'm driving along thinking about where to play Simon on Saturday," he added. "Will I use him right up front or coming forward from the midfield? Of course being so lost in thought I drove through a red light and crashed into another car."

The boys cracked up. It was typical of Jimmy. His life revolved around football. One time he hired a professional athlete to put us through our paces. The guy took us on long runs which often skirted past a stately manor. The pace he set was murderous, especially if you had a lot to drink the night before. But I soon discovered a good dodge. On the way out I would hide in a clump of bushes which surrounded the manor and on the way back, when some of the lads were struggling, I would jump out fresh as a daisy and return to Bramall Lane in the leading pack.

Despite their poor form, Sheffield United had some fine players when I was there and none better than Allan Woodward. Woodie was the best striker of a ball I've ever seen. With left or right foot he could hit the target from anywhere. He was so direct and very underestimated. Tony Currie was a joy to play alongside. He is the type of player I would pay to watch, a man with magnificent individual skills and an arrogant streak similar to Jim Baxter. Tony's party piece was nutmegging opponents. He loved making a fool of people by sticking the ball through their legs. Every time he achieved this he stuck one finger in the air. The fans adored him and it was a great shame to see his career go downhill. Currie would have been in my England XI but of course men like him and Glen Hoddle to a certain extent are looked upon as luxuries in the modern game.

Two Scots also served Sheffield well. Former Scotland centre-back Eddie Colquhoun and goalkeeper Jim Brown, who was also capped by his country, helped to shore up a shaky defence. Midfield man Davie Bradford, who was a good friend of mine, was another skilful player, who eventually left for America. Another character was Chris Calvert who was more like a film star than a footballer. With his Richard Gere looks, Chris was a constant target for women.

After a six-week lay-off following my spell in America it took me a while to reach match fitness for United. But, with this achieved, I suffered another blow one day at White Hart Lane, damaging knee ligaments against Spurs. That sidelined me for another six weeks and I was murder to live with.

Throughout my long career with Celtic I was very fortunate to avoid serious injuries. My worst scrapes came in the nightmare League Cup final against Partick Thistle when an accidental clash with Ronnie Glavin left me with six stitches in my knee, and against Hibs when I needed stitches in an ankle injury after a tackle by Jimmy O'Rourke.

When I recovered at Sheffield the team was slipping towards the Second Division but despite this I enjoyed the experience of playing in England's top tier. Their game suited my style of play. It required a slower build-up which left players with more time and space. The tackle from behind was also heavily punished, unlike in Scotland where players often took liberties.

Undoubtedly the highlight of my days in Sheffield came during my second season, when United met Fulham at Bramall Lane. George Best, Rodney Marsh and Bobby Moore were playing for the London club at the time but it was Bestie's presence which lured the fans. The match was a complete sell-out with over 40,000 turning up to see the Irish genius in action. At the risk of blowing my own trumpet I will add that yours truly was voted man of the match. Afterwards I had a good blether with Bestie in the bar. There's a mutual respect between us and George is still a good pal.

After the Fulham encounter, which gave me a brief taste of a big-time atmosphere again, it was all downhill at Sheffield. With United struggling for the second year running rumours were rife that Jimmy Sirrell was in line for the chop. I was given a free transfer at the end of a season in which the Blades managed to stay in the Second Division by the skin of their teeth. Jimmy Sirrell was very fair when he told me the news saying only: "Things haven't quite worked out, Jimmy, but we've enjoyed having you here." But, like all managers, Jimmy obviously had his spies. Reports must have filtered back regularly to him about my drinking sessions.

In hindsight I owe Jimmy an apology because I clearly gave him less than 100 per cent commitment. In the latter days we did not see eye to eye but that happens in football. It's just an occupational hazard. But overall the boss was a fair man who even invited me to his home in Nottingham a month after I arrived to share Christmas dinner with his wife and family. It was a lovely gesture because I could not get back to Scotland to be with my wife and family.

After Sheffield I was out of work for only a few days before my former Lisbon Lions team-mate Tommy Gemmell was on the phone offering to sign me for Dundee. Tam was boss at Dens Park so I jumped at the chance. But again, with the benefit of hindsight, it was a foolish move and in saying this I mean no disrespect to Dundee FC.

The players and officials made me very welcome when I arrived just in time to start pre-season training. But something bugged me right from the outset . . . it was the thought that one day I may have to face Celtic. It was a frightening prospect and one I certainly didn't relish. As the days went by and the season eventually kicked off I was in a state of panic. All I could think of was the day Dundee played Celtic. To be honest I would not have taken the park for such an occasion. My mind was made up. I would get out of it somehow. I had no other option. I would have been cheating the people of Dundee because, quite honestly, I wouldn't have tried a leg to beat Celtic. The club meant too much to me.

So to avert such a situation I had a heart-to-heart chat with big Tam and outlined my feelings and the ex-Lion was very understanding, although he himself had played against Celtic with Dundee. We agreed to part company on amicable terms. My wife was relieved. There is no way she would have settled in the city of Dundee which was another factor for my speedy departure. A permanent move to Dens Park would have meant pulling my kids away from school in Lanarkshire and that was not on. They had suffered enough disruption in Sheffield. Nevertheless, I was now in an awkward predicament. The football season was under way and I was twiddling my thumbs.

No one likes eating into their savings but I had to for a few months until Irish eyes started smiling. It was a bitter-sweet smile as I will explain later but when officials of League of Ireland club

Shelbourne offered me some competitive action I didn't hesitate. The Irish put very generous terms on the table which allowed me to fly over on the day of home games and straight back at night.

There was only one stumbling block . . . they wanted me to sign a one-year contract. Not for the first time I went to Jock Stein for advice. Stein had allowed me to train with the Celtic players at Parkhead, which was a real confidence booster. But when I approached him about the Shelbourne offer my heart missed a beat. Jock advised me to sign on a month-to-month basis. He didn't want me tied down for a year. I sniffed something in the air and asked the Big Man outright if there was still a chance of a return to Parkhead. He replied, "Wait and see", but it was enough for me. I was alive again. The thought of second time around at Parkhead filled me with the sort of expectation a young child feels on Christmas morning. I imagined the reception I would get from Celtic fans. It would have been something else and the feeling would have been mutual.

I was determined to give it my best shot in Ireland so I trained twice a day at Parkhead. Sometimes, when I spied Celtic's assistant manager Sean Fallon watching me from the stands, I ran even faster than before. In no time at all I was in good shape again and looking forward to my crucial challenge.

The Irish are famed for their hospitality and I was treated like a king in the Emerald Isle, staying at the Royal Dublin Hotel in the capital. On the field I hit top form immediately. In one game I faced former Leeds United and Eire midfield star, Johnny Giles, who was playing for Shamrock Rovers at the time. The fans raved about my performance that day and reports of my form gradually began to filter back to Scotland. There were even rumours that Sean Fallon was planning a spying trip to watch me.

At the time Celtic were going through a bad patch. They could not recapture the form of the late 1960s and early 1970s. Jock was under pressure to rekindle the glory days and maybe he saw my possible return as a morale booster for everyone. I had to believe the Big Man wanted me back. Maybe it was his final masterstroke, I thought. But one slip dashed my dreams and inevitably it was drink-related.

In Ireland I had stayed off the booze and was on my best behaviour until New Year's Eve, 1977. Shelbourne were due to play Finn Harps in Donegal. The team were staying in Ballybofey and on the eve of the game we entered into the Hogmanay spirit. A team-mate produced a bottle of Jameson's Irish Whiskey and some of the lads, including myself, polished it off. It wasn't a big bevvy

My wee gem, grand-daughter Emma.

session but word reached Celtic Park and my name was "blacked" again. I was shattered. A return to Parkhead would have been the icing on the cake. I could have died deliriously happy but a minor misdemeanour knocked me for six.

115

At the end of my stint in Ireland I was down in the dumps again. There was no way back to Celtic now, so when former Aberdeen full-back Ally Shewan offered me a deal with Elgin City I accepted. For almost a year I travelled from my home in Birkinshaw to Elgin for games.

My arrival sparked off a terrific run of success for the club who rose from mid-table to the top of the Highland League. But a severe winter put us in cold storage for four or five weeks and Elgin never recaptured the same form again.

I was very impressed with the standard of football in the Highland League. It was certainly on a par with most of the Second Division teams. And the facilities at some grounds would put some much richer clubs to shame. During my year at Elgin Billy McNeill, by this time manager of Celtic following Jock Stein's departure to Leeds United, let me train at Parkhead but I kept this in perspective. It was merely a chance to keep myself fit. Travelling to and from Elgin eventually took its toll and a few flirtations with alcohol brought about my departure.

Almost a year later — after a few minor business ventures failed — my career turned full circle when I was reinstated as a Junior with Blantyre Celtic, the team I was farmed out to when I arrived at Parkhead. But my stay with Blantyre was brief, lasting only eight weeks. During that time they also recruited former Celt Paul Wilson and the financial burden of two ex-pros proved too much for the Junior outfit to bear. It was unfair to expect too much from them so, to save any embarrassment, both Paul and I departed.

My playing days were finally over.

I've heard it said jokingly that pro players should be shot when their careers are over. They are like fish out of water. They just don't know what to do with themselves. In many ways I agree with such a sentiment. It was a really empty experience. I had been playing competitively for nearly 20 years and was lost without football.

People still ask me what I miss most. Well there's a number of things — all related to Celtic. I miss the Continental trips, the away from it all breaks at Seamill and, of course, playing in a green and white jersey. But I also miss the *camaraderie* which existed in those glorious years at Parkhead among the boys.

Quite often I recall nights at Seamill when big Jock would gather us around the fire and we would have a good laugh over a cup of tea. But I certainly don't miss the boozey days. Very soon after hanging up my boots I realised that my drinking habits would have to change. My priority became finding a job out of football to make a living for my wife and children. After three or four months down on my luck a chance meeting opened up a whole new world to me . . . the real world.

Chapter Thirteen

BUILDING A FUTURE

In many ways professional football is like a secret society. The general public rarely knows what's really going on behind the scenes and, on the inside, most players are oblivious to what is happening on the streets.

Successful players with top clubs are particularly well insulated from the harsh realities of life by thick wage packets. They live in their own little closed world and, if the profits of their labours are invested wisely, never have to experience the daily drudgery which comes with earning a crust. I was in such a privileged position for nearly 14 years, living on a cloud with money to burn. At my peak with Celtic I earned £300 a week including bonuses — "funny" money, I believe, is the colloquial term.

By rights I should have invested a large proportion of my earnings and I would strongly advise the stars of today to do so. But money had no value. There was always a constant stream of cash there to be spent . . . and spend it I did. Without doubt I could have been a millionaire by now, sitting pretty without a care in the world. But in one way or another I frittered most of my cash away. I could never see a guy stuck. Yours truly was always on hand to help some suffering soul out of a sticky situation. Barmen all over the world acquired a fair percentage of my savings and the rest went down the plughole with various business ventures.

It will come as no surprise when I reveal that Richard Branson has never asked me to go into partnership. As a businessman I was as successful as an ice cream vendor at the North Pole. My biggest investment was as a publican when I became the proud owner of the "Double J" in Hamilton but what should have been a winner turned into a financial flop.

It was a family concern and my in-laws, who helped to run the place worked tirelessly but in the end I didn't make the most of the money which came through the tills.

I committed the cardinal sin of lending my name and virtually nothing else to the venture. I should have been behind the bar all the time but I did not give enough attention to the place. It was my own mistake and I stress that no blame should be attached to anyone else.

Although I'm no longer a publican I still have lots of friends in Hamilton, so to big Dennis, the Coles, Willie Toakle, Dan Daley, Willie Bide, Joe Paterson, Paul Deacy, big Pat Somner, "The Plough" and all my former regulars I say thanks for the custom.

Various other smaller business ventures failed before I reached crisis point. With money dwindling fast I was looking down a dark tunnel. I had cut out alcohol and was doing everything else right but I was out of work. Signing on the dole never entered my head. That would have been a last resort. Then, enter the man who gave me a big break just when it was needed most.

Sean Fallon introduced me to Frank Lafferty, the well-known Glasgow building contractor, at a Celtic Supporters Club dinner in honour of Jock Stein. We got on like a house on fire and Frank invited me to be his guest at a subsequent boxing night in Glasgow. Things snowballed from there. I explained my plight carefully and two weeks later Frank offered me a job.

It was, and still is, one of the most significant moments of my life. Jimmy Johnstone, Lisbon Lion and former Scotland internationalist, had been brought back down to earth with a bump and the experience was to prove invaluable. The big money days were firmly in the past. Now I faced a battle with myself. Could I put the good times behind me and deal with the harsh realities of life on the outside?

Suddenly I was driving a lorry, picking up building supplies and delivering them to construction sites all over Scotland. At first, I must admit, it was a crushing blow to my ego. I was instantly recognised and inevitably asked the obvious question: "What are you doing here, wee man? You should have been a millionaire by now."

Of course the guys were quite right. I had experienced something which they could only dream about. For years I lived in the lap of luxury while they slaved away to keep their heads above

Signing on for Frank Lafferty.

water. But that was all history. I pulled no punches and told my workmates the truth. My wife and kids still had to be provided for, so here I was earning an honest living.

A lot of the boys felt sorry for me but I wasn't seeking pity. I just wanted to be accepted as another pair of hands. To this day I can never forget the help and support I received from all Lafferty employees. It meant more to me than most of my medals. Manual work was alien to me but there was always someone around to lend assistance when I needed it.

I make no apology for dedicating the next few paragraphs to those men and women who, in my opinion, are the salt of the earth. I offer a special vote of thanks to Willie Butterley, the man who took me under his wing, Jackie Campbell, Mr and Mrs McComb, Davie Bone, Terry Feeley and wee Stuartie, the welder. To the boys in the "bothy" — Alex, big Duncan, Jimmy Devine, Stephen and his father Willie — Gordon and Des in the office, Meg the cleaner and wee Sean the scaffolder I also say thanks.

The same sentiment is expressed to the lads from the mechanics shop, Jimmy Doc, Celtic fanatic Willie Gallagher and "Basher" Connelly, a general foreman. And a special thank you must go to Frank Lafferty, his wife Cathy and three daughters Tracey, Lorraine and Sharon, whose kindness I will always treasure. I apologise in advance to anyone I have missed.

Really, I cannot begin to measure the value of the experience gained in the construction game. After years of being closeted away in the glamorous world of football I saw the other side of the fence. The first thing I admired was the spirit of the people around me. They were never down in the dumps. No matter what kind of day they were having the boys kept plugging away. And the humour was something else!

Of course there were all the usual antics like sending a new youngster for a left-hand trowel or tartan paint. Luckily I knew all these dodges and was well prepared for any wind-up. But one thing I experienced for the first time was the "sub". To me a sub was the guy who sat on the bench during a football match. But in Glasgow parlance it is something quite different . . . an advance on your wages. It never ceased to amaze me how many guys borrowed £10, £20 or more on a Monday morning and paid it back out of their wage packets on Friday. I couldn't work the logic of such a move but it was a real cottage industry!

Pay-day was another eye-opener for me. As far as production was concerned, Friday was virtually a non-event. The workforce arrived in the morning and did as little as possible before collecting

Some of the Lafferty team.

their wages and beating a hasty retreat. It seemed like an accepted practice and I'm sure even Frank Lafferty would agree.

During my football career Friday was just the day before a game, there was nothing special about it. But in the "real" world Friday was the day for letting your hair down (a hard task for me) after a mundane week. Everyone came alive. It was like having Hogmanay every week and, predictably, a lot of talk centred on football. Some of the banter between Celtic and Rangers fans was hilarious and I lapped it up. The rivalry was intense but it was all good clean fun.

Working with and watching these guys completely changed my attitude towards football fans and Celtic fans in particular. Don't get me wrong, I always appreciated the backing from the Parkhead terracings but, like all players past and present, I did not realise the sacrifices punters made to cheer on their favourite team. At Lafferty's, some men sweated their guts out just to get away early for a Celtic match at Aberdeen. The same guys travelled all over the country on a Saturday to support the club and then worked overtime on a Sunday in order to get time off for another game in midweek. On a Sunday morning some of them would fall asleep in the bothy at tea-break through exhaustion.

Such loyalty was staggering and made me feel humble. I mention these facts mainly for the benefit of present-day players. I'm not implying that players are thoughtless — many of them do sterling work for charity and visit hospitals regularly to pep up sick children, which I admire. But perhaps they don't realise, as I didn't, the sacrifices some fans willingly make. Ultimately the punters pay the players' wages and players should never forget this.

Working with Frank Lafferty's firm and rubbing shoulders with his fine set of employees for three years is a very fond memory. It taught me all about the obstacles facing the ordinary working man who endures hardship from 8 a.m. to 5 p.m. at least five days a week with a smile on his face most of the time. It was a happy time in a world far removed from the "grab what you can" days at Sheffield.

But in terms of hard labour it was nothing compared to my next step into the unknown as a general labourer with John Keane, a gas contractor from Edinburgh. This really made me appreciate that I had been wrapped in cotton wool for 14 years at Celtic Park. John, a genial Irishman, helped me out of a spot after I left my job with Frank Lafferty.

For almost a year I worked, mainly in Kirkcaldy, digging test holes for gas pipes along the seafront of the Fife town, only minutes away from Willie Johnston's public house. Come hail, rain, frost or snow the rest of the lads and I were out, wrapped in oilskins, with picks and shovels digging holes, spreading tar and refilling the same holes. It was back-breaking work with no hiding place and it took its toll. After being exposed to the elements once too often I was laid up with 'flu for three weeks. It was a welcome respite. Often when I came home from work I could barely raise my hands above my head — and I thought a training session under Jock Stein had been murder!

Every morning I was picked up in a van at 6.30 a.m. by an old friend, Willie Donaldson, a general foreman with Keane. Willie is a great character and I owe him a lot for looking after me in those early days when the going was rough. But again, just like at Lafferty's, the whole squad treated me tremendously and couldn't do enough to help. I thank them all for their assistance.

The lads even taught me to use a jackhammer and by the end of the year I was a dab hand with the tool. Looking back, I only wish I had possessed one of them in 1974 when Celtic met Atletico

Doing my bit for charity.

Madrid in the infamous European Cup semi-final. Maybe then we would have sorted out those savage Spaniards!

It was during my time as a labourer in Kirkcaldy I took on the part-time post as coach of Celtic's new under-18 side, an episode in my life which I have charted elsewhere in this book. In many ways life was more straightforward delivering cement or digging holes. At least the people around me were genuine, unlike a few characters I've met.

For the past nine months I've been employed as a full-time salesman for ELN Communications in Rosyth, selling satellite TV dishes all around Scotland. It's an enjoyable job which offers a real chance to make a good living for my wife and children and, as I've said, that is my number one priority.

Inevitably, I am still quizzed today about my fall from grace in football. People ask me if I have regrets about my past and of course drinking is certainly the main one. Thankfully, today I can have a drink like the next man without going over the top. I suppose I have learned my lesson the hard way.

Otherwise I can't really complain. For 14 years I lived out a dream by playing for Celtic. Football gave me the chance to see places which the average man can only look at in holiday brochures. It allowed me to attain honours which every father would like to see his son attain. And it brought me riches which only top-flight businessmen could match.

In many ways every day was a bonus when I look at my pals on building sites. Now these guys really could complain about their lot in life but from experience I know that most of them grin and bear it. It would be an insult to them for me to do otherwise.

Chapter Fourteen

IT'S A FUNNY OLD GAME

Over the years football has given me more laughs than a battery of stand-up comedians. In my era the game was littered with jokers who could have made careers for themselves on the stage. And amusing incidents were ten a penny.

Maybe the fun flows in football because professional players travel all over the world and are often cooped up in strange locations abroad or letting their hair down in exotic spots after a long, hard season. But, for whatever reason, football can rival the light entertainment industry for laughs any time. I enjoy a good giggle so here is a collection of my favourite anecdotes and incidents from the past 20 years.

Inevitably, some of the best laughs have been at my expense. A classic example was back in the Lisbon era when Celtic played a pre-season friendly in Vienna against a local minor side. On the morning of the game I felt unwell. It must have been something I'd eaten because for the next few hours I was running back and forth to the loo. I kept my personal problem to myself but the game was only minutes old when disaster struck . . . the dreaded dose of diarrhoea had returned. I was in a state of panic. What could I do? There was literally no time to lose. I couldn't alert the referee or the bench to my predicament so I just took off.

The game was being played on the equivalent of a public park with lots of football pitches. I had to run across another pitch where a match was in progress. Luckily, after a few agonising moments, I found a public toilet, just before a nasty accident happened. The feeling of sheer relief was unbelievable.

Contestants for the Parkhead knobbly knees competition — O'Neill, Lennox, Murdoch and Johnstone — arrive back from training at Barrowfield.

By this time assistant manager Sean Fallon had realised something was amiss as he counted the players on the park. Celtic had only ten men. Other players, who noticed me taking off into the distance, were completely baffled by what they saw as my massive brainstorm but I had no time to explain on my return to the action. At half time in the dressing-room the rest of the lads quizzed me on my double-quick disappearing act and on hearing the hilarious explanation they almost took the roof off laughing. The opposition next door must have felt we were not treating them very seriously!.

That was the second time bodily functions had left me in an embarrassing situation. The first came a few years previously, just as I was making a name for myself with Celtic.

I'm no lover of the high life but one night I was out for a meal with my friend Frank Cairney of Celtic Boys' Club in a posh Glasgow restaurant. I was really self-conscious. This wasn't my scene and I felt so uncomfortable. All evening I tried, unsuccessfully, to attract a waiter's attention by making what can only be described as a "pissing" noise. Eventually, seeing my plight, an acutely embarrassed Frank explained that this wasn't the way to do it. All I needed to do, said Frank, was to look straight at a waiter, catch his attention, and then nod my head and he would come over in due course.

This worked a treat and by the end of the night I felt an apology was in order to the harassed waiter. But, excuse the pun, I made a meal of this. Before leaving the restaurant I called the guy over and, stumbling for words, spluttered: "Sorry for pissing at you earlier, sir." The poor waiter and Frank didn't know what to say or where to look. Needless to say we made a quick exit after that.

Frank has been my straight-man on a few other occasions. One Sunday afternoon we took a trip to the Glasgow "Barras" to buy pop records. I loved music and would often buy a dozen LPs at a time. By now I was instantly recognised as Jimmy Johnstone, the Celtic star. Naturally people came up for autographs and I duly obliged. But at one point I was standing against an empty stall for a breather when this lovely old "Glesca" wifie, corned beef legs and all, came up to me and said: "Son, dae you mind if I put my bundle on your barra for a wee minute? I'm puffed oot."

Quick as a flash I replied: "Aye, it's OK missus. I'm no doing much today anyway." It was a lovely little moment which helped to keep my feet on the ground.

Another time Frank accompanied me to Parkhead where I was due a dressing down from the directors for stepping out of line. We

Square-bashing with Neilly Mochan leading the line.

were sitting in the foyer waiting to be called and looking at pictures of Celtic "greats" on the walls. Both of us were uptight but I turned to Frank and quipped: "Do you think I'll ever get my photo up there?" We both laugh about that now although at the time it was a deadly serious matter.

Well, that's enough about me for the moment. I must tell you about a really funny character — my old pal Willie Henderson of Rangers. Willie, like myself, got up to some amazing antics during his career. My favourite story about him came when he was playing for Rangers in Russia and rooming with Ronnie McKinnon.

The Soviets can't get enough of Western gear. They love capitalist clothes like jeans and teeshirts. One night Ronnie, who was sleeping, awoke to find Willie and a stranger sitting at the bottom of his bed. Through bleary eyes Ronnie saw his team-mate and a little Russian hawker rifling through his case. Willie was flogging off some of Ronnie's best gear! When confronted by

Ronnie on what he was doing wee Willie replied: "I'm just trying to make us a few extra bob, big man."

Willie was unbeatable. Nothing put him off. During another Russian trip the story goes that he tried to telephone his fiancée Mary Bell back home. But she wasn't on the phone! This didn't deter Willie who rang up a public telephone box in the little Lanarkshire village of Greengairs. Getting through to Scotland was a big enough achievement but Willie really came up trumps when a passer-by picked up the phone. The wee man asked the stranger to go to a certain house and get Mary to the blower, which he duly did. Of course her family needed a lot of convincing that this wasn't one big wind-up.

On another occasion Willie was walking along Sauchiehall Street in Glasgow when a young girl approached him. Willie prepared himself for a compliment but a shock lay in store. The girl snapped: "God, you're even uglier than I thought." Willie took this on the chin and recounted the story when he reached Ibrox for training. And his punchline was a beauty. While looking in a dressing-room mirror, he turned to his buddy Jim Baxter and said: "You know, Jim, I was thinking of suing that wee bitch but she wasn't far wrong."

Rangers striker George McLean was another irrepressible character. Big "Dandy" was a master of the one-liner. Back in the 1960s Rangers were whipped 6-1 by Real Madrid. After the game the players were all making excuses for their performances. They blamed everything from the referee to the pitch. When asked what he thought of the pitch Dandy replied: "The spot I was standing on was OK."

After another beating George was singled out for fierce criticism by the Rangers boss at the time, Scot Symon. Symon tore into the striker and blazed: "That's the worst performance I've ever seen from a Rangers player." Most players would have crumbled but big George casually retorted: "There's plenty more where that one came from, boss."

Of course, as I've said, close-season tours or holidays offered tremendous scope for gathering comic cuts. I could write another book on the funny moments of the Lisbon era alone.

One of the great characters was Celtic trainer Neilly Mochan. During those days, no matter where we travelled abroad, Jock Stein believed that after a long flight the players should be sent on a 20-minute run to stretch their legs after checking into a hotel. Neilly was put in charge of the pack and these runs became known as "Mochan's Manoeuvres". Most of the time Neilly hadn't a clue about where he was going. He always wandered off the beaten track and rarely stuck to main roads. Twenty minutes turned into an hour and a half. Bertie Auld was always winding Neilly up by shouting: "Which way now, Neilly?" Neilly would just shove up a hand and point anywhere. Once in Italy we ended up in a vineyard and were chased by a farmer and two ferocious dogs. What a scatter it was as players hared off in all directions. We had a few choice words for Neilly that night!

The Big Man loved to hear our accounts of these wayward runs when we arrived back at the hotel shattered and sore. "Another classic, gaffer," I would chirp as the Boss doubled up with laughter.

Often at Hampden, our second home in those heady days, the boys would wind Neilly up about the goal he scored in the Coronation Cup back in 1953. Someone would say: "Here's the spot, isn't it, Neilly?" But our loyal trainer shrugged this aside, grabbed my arm and marched 20 yards further from goal, commenting: "I'll show you, James." Of course the distance increased every few months and Neilly always added that the goal was scored in heavy rain with a big brown ball which weighed a ton.

My other favourite Neilly tale came from Israel where we were taking a well-earned close-season break one year. Neilly was sitting at the pool rubbing olive oil into his massive thighs — they were like tree trunks — while saying to the lads: "This gets the tan on you, by the way." I got the impression he hadn't been away on a holiday before. The following day Neilly was a sight for sore eyes. He could barely get his trousers on. His legs were swollen and red raw with sunburn. To look at him walking you would have thought he was wearing two "stookies".

Talking of Israel and sunburn reminds me of another time we stayed outside Tel Aviv in a beautiful country club during a summer break. After landing, some of the lads, myself included, went to a club for a good bevvy. This was an accepted practice during an end-of-season holiday. The first thing we heard was a voice in the background welcoming us: "Hey, you shower of Scots b-------." It was Alan Ball, on his own. Ballie's team-mates had arrived over a week earlier and were well and truly shattered after one long binge. But Ballie had been on England duty and had just jetted in. Needless to say he was looking for a good drink. Alan was great fun. His patter was spot-on and that little croaking voice just topped it off.

At the end of the night we were all well and truly blitzed when Ballie suggested that we jump into some taxis and go back to meet

If the pilot's with us who's flying the plane, boys?

the rest of the Everton lads. Well, it seemed like a good idea at the time! But, to be honest, the Goodison lads could have lived without a bunch of Scottish drunks knocking them up at 3 a.m. A blitzed Ballie introduced us to Joe Royle and his other team-mates, who politely shook hands before returning to bed.

Bobby Lennox and I made a date to meet Ballie two nights later which turned out to be another mistake. The following day I overdid the "macho man" bit and ended up with serious sunburn. It was about 100 degrees in the shade and, being red-haired and fair-skinned, I should have known better than to lie in the sun for hours. That reckless action put me in bed for two days and I missed out on trips to Jerusalem and the Wailing Wall (I suppose I was the Weeping Wally).

The next night I was lying in bed, shaking like a leaf and up to my neck in cream when there was a knock on the door. I turned to my room-mate "Lemon" who drew me a blank look. We had forgotten completely about the arrangement with Ballie. On opening the door I was met by a boozed-up Ballie who cursed us both upside down for leaving him in the lurch. "I thought you buggers were coming to meet me," he croaked. "I was left on my own surrounded by all those bloody Israelis." At that moment the Big Man appeared. I feared the worst from the Boss but he merely pacified Alan and led him away to a taxi.

Jock wasn't always so easy-going. I remember a time when

Celtic were in Jersey for a testimonial match. One night Jock found Bertie, big Tommy Gemmell and some other lads drinking secretly in a room. Funnily enough, I wasn't there, which must have been a first. Jock stormed into the room, lifted a bottle of Vodka and numerous bottles of Coke and threw it all in the bath before storming off in a rage.

The boys sat shellshocked for seconds before Bertie ran through to the bathrom to examine the damage. As luck would have it, everything had shattered except the Vodka bottle but Bertie was restrained from chasing after the Big Man to give him the good news!

Jock blew his top again when Celtic were in Amsterdam to play Ajax and Jim Brogan was the poor soul on the receiving end. On the night before the game a bunch of players and Jock were sitting in the foyer of the Amsterdam Hilton when the Big Man spied a waiter heading towards a lift with a tray laden with soft drinks and a big glass of sherry, topped off with cherries.

Without a word of a lie, Jock got off his seat and followed the waiter into the lift. The Dutchman must have been baffled as Jock tracked his every step until he reached his last port of call . . . the room with the occupant who liked sherry. The Big Man was literally breathing down the waiter's neck as the door was opened by Brogie.

Now Jim was never a big drinker. He valued his fitness too much but he did like the occasional sherry before bedtime. Unfortunately, he was also a forthright character who rarely backed down, even when in a corner. Jim thanked the waiter before being hit with a verbal barrage from the Big Man who demanded an explanation for the sherry order. Instead of owning up to an honest mistake Brogie tried to make a case for himself and proceeded to tell Jock that at home he always had a sherry before going to bed. Inevitably, it cut no ice with Jock who showered him with expletives before laying down the law. Sherry was out of bounds for Brogie from then on.

I must admit the rest of the boys had a good laugh when Jim told the story the next morning. Laughing helped to ease the pressure which was never far away when playing for Celtic.

I was never a joker like wee Bertie or Big Tam. Bobby Lennox and I were just noise-up merchants. We would do daft things like come down early before meals and hide all the salt and pepper pots. Sometimes, if another player was engaged in conversation at the table, we would catch the eye of a waitress and whisper: "He's not allowed that." The said player would then sit around waiting

Definitely not Ben Hur. Me and wee Willie horsing around.

for a succulent steak which never came.

Bobby and I were also banned from the card schools for causing mayhem and only got on the golf course after a struggle. Neither of us could swing a club very effectively but we loved putting the others off. I suppose we had the same silly sense of humour.

I would like to round off with a couple of stories about one of Celtic's greatest players and a personal favourite of mine, Charlie Tully. Tales about him are still told today at Parkhead. The Irish legend was one of the few who was allowed to call Robert Kelly, as he was then, "Bob".

The story goes that during one tour in the 1950s some Celtic players were complaining about the amount of spending money they had been given. Tully, who was one of the bunch, was elected as the man to confront Robert Kelly on the issue and he readily agreed. He strolled downstairs and interrupted a conversation

134

between the directors in the hotel foyer. The other players eagerly leaned over the first-floor balcony to catch Charlie's short speech which went something like this. "Bob, some of the boys are complaining about the lack of spending money but to be honest I think they are being greedy. I think you've been very fair." The crafty Irishman had landed his team-mates in it just for a laugh!

My last anecdote comes, appropriately enough, from Jock Stein. The Big Man told me about Tully's funeral in Belfast which he attended with Sean Fallon, Jimmy Farrell, Neilly Mochan and John Bonner. The crowds were phenomenal and people were hanging out of windows to catch a glimpse of the funeral cortège. The Celtic officials were following behind in a taxi and at one point John Bonner turned to Jock and said: "You know, Jock, Charlie would have loved this." It was an Irish joke but in many ways it was probably true.

Chapter Fifteen

MUSIC AND MEGASTARS

The world of rock music has had a narrow escape because if I hadn't made a name for myself on the football park nothing would have given me more pleasure than becoming a pop star!

Maybe it's too mind-boggling to imagine but at one time I loved the thought of singing live in front of screaming thousands. Music has always been my biggest passion apart from football and there are similarities between both industries. Rock artists and football players all have a stage on which to perform and entertain fans. But perhaps it's a blessing in disguise that I didn't master the guitar at an early age because a rock star's lifestyle may have killed me!

Today I content myself by listening to my favourite bands like the Beatles, the Rolling Stones, U2 and Queen. I also admire individuals like Elton John, Rod Stewart and my pal Frankie Miller. Frankie is one of the best "blues" singers in the world and I could listen to his rasping, lived-in voice all night long. Despite his success in the United States, Frankie is fiercely proud of his Glasgow background — and he's also a big Celtic fan.

When I owned a public house in Hamilton he turned up one night and struck a bargain with me. Frankie offered to sing a few numbers for the regulars if I gave him one of my Celtic strips. It was a fair deal because my buddy brought the house down and, as far as I know, he still wears the green and white jersey occasionally on tour.

Like Frankie, Rod Stewart is a real down-to-earth guy. I met him for the first time back in the early 1970s when he visited Celtic

On song with Rod Stewart, Kenny Dalglish, Dixie Deans and Co.

Park for a photo session. Afterwards a few of the lads, including myself, invited him along for a few pints and he spent most of the night talking about football before rushing off to Edinburgh. The next time we met up was in 1974 at the World Cup finals in West Germany. On the night we were put out by Yugoslavia the lads had a farewell party and Rod, who is a great friend of Denis Law's, got up on stage and sang a few numbers completely unaccompanied. I thought that took a lot of courage.

Football has certainly given me the opportunity to meet many so-called megastars and it's nice to know that most of them are just ordinary guys off stage. Take Billy Connolly for instance. During a public performance the "Big Yin" is unflappable but I remember one occasion when he let his guard down. It was just before the 1974 World Cup finals and the Scotland party were preparing at Largs. Billy, who was just coming to the fore then, came along to our hotel one night to give us an impromptu show. As the lads

Cuffed again by the Lawman.

gathered around the little makeshift stage the "Big Yin" announced: "I've never been so nervous in my life. I'm here to entertain you but you guys are all my heroes. What do I dae?" But within minutes Billy had us holding our sides with his inimitable patter. From that night on I became firm friends with the Big Yin and since then he has stayed at my house in Birkinshaw a few times.

Billy is a big football fan, just like 007, Sean Connery. I met the former James Bond back in 1967 at Hampden Park when Celtic played the first leg of their infamous World Club Championship tie against Racing Club of Argentina. What struck me immediately was the man's physique. He was enormous. I will never forget his comments to the players after the rough-house match. Sean, a big Celtic supporter, breezed into the dressing-room and said: "I've got to hand it to you boys. I couldn't have kept my head out there. I'm afraid I would have broken a few jaws." Perhaps Celtic should have drafted in James Bond for the return leg!

Incidentally, Sean is one of my favourite actors. On the sporting front I also have my favourites away from football. Top of the list must be Muhammad Ali in his heyday. In my opinion there will never be a showman like him in the fight game, although I feel even the "greatest" would have struggled against the current world heavyweight champion Mike Tyson. This guy's power is awesome and I wouldn't like to come within 100 miles of him. Thankfully, my fear of flying should see to that! Sugar Ray Leonard was another star performer. He had every punch in the book and the style to go with it.

Among my other favourite sports is tennis. I often played the game during my football career for relaxation. My all-time favourite stars are Bjorn Borg and Ilie Nastase. I admired Borg's ice-cool temperament and, although Nastase was a bit of a hot-head, his touch was second to none. John McEnroe gets up my nose. His tantrums are completely out of order. Admittedly, I was a fiery character on the park but it was usually just a split-second reaction. I never purposefully went out to be offensive but "Superbrat" seems to thrive on this sort of behaviour.

Talking of my temper, people often point out that I was ordered off six times in my career and booked on countless other occasions. I'm not condoning those actions but really it was just part of my make-up. At one point I asked a doctor for advice on how to cure my temper but he offered no remedy. For a while I tried hypnosis on the night before a game and this certainly relaxed me.

Snooker ace Alex Higgins is a man famed for his temper and

Living it up in my Jag.

tantrums but I must admit I prefer him and Jimmy White to Steve Davis. Higgins and White are men with individual styles which excite the fans. They are value for money merchants.

But perhaps the sportsmen I admire most are golfers because the vast majority of them are so gracious even in defeat. It's easy to be a good winner but a lot more difficult to swallow disappointment and shake hands after a defeat. Other sportsmen could learn a thing or two about fair play from men like Jack Nicklaus and Arnold Palmer. It's a pity neither of them were around in Lanarkshire a few years back when I was bitten by the golfing bug. As a Celtic player money was no object so I bought clubs, bags, brolly, trolley, balls, the lot, and during one long, hot summer I burned up Bothwell Golf Club with some friends. But, while I enjoy a round of golf, I will never make Nick Faldo shake in his boots.

My latest craze is American Football — although I hasten to add watching it and not playing. Luckily I'm too small anyway, but all the money in the world would not convince me to don shoulder pads and headgear and do battle with these bruisers. Without doubt it's the toughest sport around. Nevertheless, I enjoy watching the quarterbacks in action. Some of them can pass a ball as well as Bobby Murdoch or Bertie Auld.

Away from sport I enjoy nothing more than a good Indian meal. I'm virtually addicted to the stuff! For the past 15 years I have gone to the best Indian restaurant in Glasgow, the Shenaz in Berkeley Street. I suppose you could say I've been currying favour with the manager!

Chapter Sixteen

GET BACK TO BASICS
— I'M BORED!

I'm often asked what football lacks today and I usually sum it up in one word — individuals. Don't get me wrong. I'm not just another ex-pro having a cheap pot-shot at modern-day players. I just happen to believe that football is a completely different ball game now than in my era.

The punters who pay money to stand on the terracings still want to be entertained but they are being sold short these days. There is a win-at-all-costs attitude running through the game and this is a very dangerous trend. It starts at grassroots level where kids are asked to play competitively at far too young an age. Instead of being allowed to express themselves, youngsters are asked to fit into a system. Their heads are filled with tactics and coaches' mumbo-jumbo. Developing individual skills is a side issue. Victory is the be-all and end-all.

Television helps to perpetuate the myth that football is all about organisation and rigid formats. More games than ever before are beamed into homes and youngsters mimic their heroes who play in 4-2-4 or 4-3-3 formations.

Modern managers are often afraid to introduce flair and imagination to their teams because of the cut-throat pressures which now exist in the pro game. Taking a chance with a young talent could cost a boss his job so most don't take the risk. I strongly believe we must go back to basics and give kids enough rope to become individuals in their own right on the park. Let them enjoy themselves at nine, ten or 11 years old. Surely it's a crime to harness youth and stifle freedom of expression.

The perfect advert for summer soccer

In my younger days I loved doing my own thing on the park. I always wanted to hold the ball for a while and show some fancy footwork. I might have overdone it sometimes but I learned from my mistakes. Youngsters won't learn basic technical skills if they are asked to virtually ignore the ball and concentrate on marking space or closing down an opponent.

My advice to managers is not to curb natural talent. Encourage players to try the unexpected just like the greatest manager of all, Jock Stein. Jock motivated us and made us tactically aware of the opposition but I will always remember his favourite phrase before a game: "When you cross that line it's up to you. I'm non-existent." The Big Man always appreciated that players "did the business". Of course a team needs a figurehead or manager and Jock was the best but it was the guys who stripped for action who mattered most. In training we would practise a set move maybe 100 times but it was

143

seldom brought into use on the pitch. Everything came down to pure instinct from individuals. Our game was based on attack and taking men on. It wasn't a cavalry charge but, while we were going forward, the opposition could not pose a threat. "Use your ability to the full," said the Big Man. Billy McNeill and all other managers should commit those words to memory.

Negative thinking should be banned. Kids should, quite literally, vote with their feet and practise the art of individualism. Simple exercises can develop skills which may be lurking just beneath the surface. Improve the bad foot — the one used for standing on. Most players have one. If you can head well on one side, concentrate on the other. Trap the ball, take it on the chest and knee at any pace. Control it and turn on a sixpence. Do all this and you will be one step ahead of the rest — technically superior.

I recall an interview with Kevin Keegan in which he said he improved as a player after signing for Hamburg in West Germany. The Continentals concentrate much more on technique than the Scots or English. And while our game will always be more entertaining than down south it is not based on skill. Most British defenders, for instance, are very limited on the ground although there are worthy exceptions, like Liverpool's Mark Lawrenson and Willie Miller of Aberdeen. Often defenders are not to blame. They are instructed to belt the ball up the park pronto. This hit-and-hope approach frustrates strikers.

You never see this tactic adopted by Brazil for instance. In fact by spying on a Brazilian camp it is impossible to tell who is a defender or an attacker. They are all so comfortable on the ball, just like Frenchmen Platini and Tigana or Denmark's brilliant young striker Michael Laudrup. Of course even they can't match magical Diego Maradona. I'm a sucker for his talent — I would pay £10 million to keep him in my team. What an asset! He would be worth such a huge outlay because the little Argentinian pulls in crowds. There would always be a return on the investment.

The same could be said for my three favourite individuals from these shores. Firstly, there was George Best. His individual skills were out of this world. Nobody could live with him when he turned on the tricks. I loved to see him tormenting defenders. He would feign a shot and bodies would fall all over the place. His touch was different class. George was also very brave. I was often surprised by the amount of tackles he won. He never shirked a challenge. A true genius.

Jimmy Greaves was my favourite finisher although I hasten to add he was around just before my time. No one could match his coolness in a one-to-one situation with a goalkeeper. To be able to

A spot of target practice.

control every emotion and nonchalantly stick the ball away like Greavsie is not easy. Believe me, I've been in that situation a few times and it's frightening. But Jimmy was magnificent under pressure. He rarely cracked the ball into the net.

Denis Law was a similiar sort of player but sharper over a five-yard burst. Denis did most of his damage in the six-yard box. He was more aggressive than Greavsie but possessed the same gift for sticking the ball in the net.

Scotland's domestic game has in relatively recent years also produced some men who were a bit special in front of goal. Men

145

like Ralph Brand, Jim Forrest and Jimmy Millar. Another personal favourite, although not a striker, was Ian McMillan, the wee general. Then there was Willie Johnston, one of the best Rangers players I've ever seen. On his game Willie was outstanding and his pace was electrifying. Nobody could live with it. Willie could give opponents five yards of a start and then fly past them down the left flank. I didn't like to see him on song against Celtic because it always spelled trouble.

Of course that was back in the days before the advent of the Premier League. I must confess I'm no fan of this particular set-up . . . *it must be boring to play in.* I'm sure, if pressed, most Scottish players would agree with this statement. How can you play each other at least four times a season and make it interesting for the public? Players must know each other inside out. If I was around today I'm sure I would be well versed in opponents' weaknesses after one season. It might be competitive but to me it's a sham. There is still an élite who compete for the title and the rest face a constant fight to avoid the dreaded drop.

In many ways it's not much different from the old-style First Division and at least in those days players and fans got the opportunity to visit more grounds and face more opponents. OK, I know the argument that teams like Celtic hammered the likes of Stirling Albion and Arbroath. But I don't strictly go along with that. We may have won, even won well on occasions, but I recall even the great Lisbon Lions getting on some sticky wickets at smaller grounds. To the minor clubs a meeting with Celtic or Rangers was a pay day which would probably keep them afloat for the rest of the season. But it was also a cup final to them. Players would raise their game against the Old Firm and on a tight pitch with an electric atmosphere on the terracings, anything could happen.

Even Jock Stein admitted that the hardest thing for Celtic to do was play a big European tie at Parkhead in midweek and then visit a small town team on the Saturday. We were on a hiding to nothing. Defeat brought acute embarrassment and even victory was treated as a hollow achievement unless the opposition had been well and truly hammered.

In saying all this I'm not advocating a return to the old system. I think those days have gone but I also feel the Premier League's days are numbered. The logical progression, which will come sooner rather than later in my opinion, is a *British* league. I think it is inevitable. I feel the punters want it and although the top clubs are playing their cards close to their chests most of them know it's the only way forward.

With the master . . . Sir Stanley Matthews.

Money talks in football just like anywhere else and I'm sure Celtic, Rangers, Aberdeen, Hearts, Hibs and Dundee United have estimated the amount of cash which could roll in from meeting England's top contenders. Surely it would be a mouth-watering prospect for Scottish clubs and their supporters to have Manchester United, Liverpool, Arsenal, Spurs, Everton, Newcastle or Nottingham Forest playing on their grounds every second week. With all due respect, it must be more appealing than facing the like of Falkirk, Morton and Dunfermline week in week out.

Of course such a move would decimate Scottish football. Some clubs would probably go to the wall but, at the risk of sounding heartless, maybe there are too many clubs in Scotland anyway at the moment. The rich clubs prop up the minnows. It's always been that way. A meeting with Celtic or Rangers can keep a smaller club going for a season, as I've said. But I suppose it's a case of "What price progress?"

Fans could be balloted on the idea but it would be like block voting with trade unions. The big boys always hold the balance of power. A breakaway would leave the smaller clubs with no star names but for the clubs which survived it might provide a chance to rear young talent away from the pressures of living in the shadows of Celtic, Rangers, Aberdeen and Hearts. Perhaps it could be stipulated that the top clubs would have to play in the Scottish Cup each season. It's a possibility. Whichever way you look at it a British League would benefit the best players. It would give them the chance to compete against the top men in the UK all of the time.

Outwith Celtic and Rangers there are few individuals with star quality in the Scottish game. One of my personal favourites is Paul Sturrock of Dundee United. I admire his ability to turn an opponent in much the same way as Kenny Dalglish. Paul is a seasoned campaigner and a very good professional who has watched his fitness over the years. I would pay money to watch him.

I'm also a big fan of Rangers' Iain Ferguson who has been bred in the modern mould. He is big and strong but possesses some lovely ball skills. It speaks volumes that Rangers were prepared to spend such an amount to sign him.

Young John Collins of Hibs is also worth a king's ransom. It's no secret how much I admire the youngster but I feel he may have to leave Hibs and perform on a bigger stage to fulfil his undoubted potential. Charlie Nicholas is another individual whom I have already spoken about at length.

That inevitably brings me around to the Old Firm. Celtic are certainly blessed with some superb individuals in Joe Miller, Paul McStay and Andy Walker but I must add Tommy Burns to that list. Tommy is now in the twilight of his career. He has been dogged by injury over the years, but there are still few better ball players in the Scottish game. Tommy is a pleasure to watch and it's obvious what the fans think of him after the amazing turnout at his testimonial match against Liverpool earlier this season. Tommy is also a true Celtic man at heart and I take my hat off to him for his loyalty to the club.

Without doubt the best striker in the land is Ally McCoist of

Rangers. The boy has proved his worth this season by consistently hitting the target. And that is easier said than done because of the nature of a Premier League where clubs have become so accustomed to each other. Super Ally is very sharp and I admire the way he stuck to the task after getting a rough ride from Rangers fans a few seasons ago.

His team-mate Ian Durrant is a youngster who would grace any team. He has tremendous potential and seems to have settled down at Ibrox again after a stormy time last season when he looked set to leave. Of course he is just a part of the rich and powerful Rangers who have made the rest of Britain sit up and take notice of Scottish football. I think even the most biased Celtic fan would admit that the Ibrox men have breathed fresh life into the game north of the border by their amazing spending spree. They upped the ante for everyone and Celtic, Aberdeen, Hearts and even Hibs joined in.

Rangers have splashed out a fortune to assemble virtually a new team but two of their purchases stand head and shoulders above the rest in my opinion. When Chris Woods was signed for nearly £650,000 from Norwich a lot of eyebrows were raised. It was a lot of cash for a goalkeeper but Woods has certainly proved to be value for money. His shut-out record is exceptional, although a big contributory factor to this is the other inspired signing, Terry Butcher. Butcher is a first-class defender and his presence has shored up a previously leaky rearguard. The England centre-back is also a very commanding figure on and off the park, an ideal captain and ambassador for the club.

I must also say a word about Mark Walters, the first black player to appear in Scotland. Walters took some stick in his early days at Ibrox from people with the cheek to call themselves football supporters. But he has shrugged it all off and won people over with his ball skills. Again I go back to the word individual. Walters entertains the fans and, consequently, they come back for more.

Attendances in the Premier League are currently very healthy but only for four clubs — Rangers, Celtic, Hearts and Aberdeen. The rest struggle to make ends meet and are a world removed from the ritzy lifestyles of Parkhead, Ibrox, Pittodrie or Tynecastle. And the provincial "paupers" subsequently cannot compete on the transfer market so it's a Catch 22 situation.

Talking of transfers, I must offer a word of warning to the élite who are now paying over the odds for players. Wildly inflated transfer fees do the game no good at all because one day the bubble bursts and clubs are left in a deep hole.

On the international front many people feel Scotland are

Best of friends. A night out with old buddies Willie Henderson and George Best.

emerging from a big hole but I'm not convinced yet. For a start I don't know if Andy Roxburgh is the right man for the manager's job. In saying this I'm not trying to bring the man down. I just have reservations about his lack of experience for such an important

150

Getting back to the basics — ball control Jinky-style.

post. Roxburgh has not been in charge of a top team before and had some hard acts to follow in Jock Stein and Alex Ferguson.

Andy Roxburgh's biggest problem will be winning respect from players. I don't care what anyone says to the contrary, if a manager doesn't get respect he can forget it. And respect is usually gained from results in the past at club level. Roxburgh doesn't have a history at club level so his job is even more difficult.

Most critics feel we are now on the right lines at international level but I will reserve judgement until we achieve something significant. Last year we defeated Bulgaria in Sofia but the horse had bolted by then, so to speak. We had already failed to qualify for the European Championships so the game was meaningless. I will judge Scotland on results when the chips are down, in the World Cup qualifying ties. Then we will see what Roxburgh is really made of. He certainly has a good pool of players around him, a mixture of youth and experience, but of course we miss the presence of a Dalglish or Souness. McStay has emerged as a successor to Souness and I can see him setting the world on fire with men like Mo Johnston, revitalised since his move to Nantes, around him. Of course McStay and Johnston have been part of the international scene for some years since their days together at Parkhead.

151

I've always felt it was easier for players from big clubs to adapt to the Scotland scene (although I had my difficulties). They usually have clubmates around in the squad so the atmosphere is no different from every other day of the week. It's not always so easy for a player from a provincial club who may be mixing with the "big noises" for the first time. He can take a while to settle in. I know this from my days with Scotland. And of course he hears all the talk about the money which can be earned elsewhere in Scotland or south of the border. It can be an unnerving experience but if the guy is a strong enough individual he will overcome the psychological barrier and make a name for himself. But there I go talking about individuals again. Let's stop talking about them and go out and breed some. That way football will be an entertainment rather than an endurance test.

Chapter Seventeen
THE RAMPANT LIONS REVISITED

Last year I had the pleasure of revisiting one of my favourite spots, the little town of Seamill on the Ayrshire coast. The reason for the nostalgic trip was to take part in an hour-long programme being filmed by Scottish Television. The subjects of the show were ten very special men and myself . . . the Lisbon Lions.

From the moment the boys were reunited at the Scottish Television studios in Cowcaddens, Glasgow, the champagne flowed. The journey along the long and winding roads to Seamill was a laugh-a-minute affair. And as the cameras rolled we amassed enough material to put a five-part comedy series on the air. Unfortunately, some of it — the bits which had people rolling in the aisles — was too near the bone for transmission and finished on the cutting-room floor. But it was all off the cuff, just like the style of play which captured the attention of the world back in 1967.

Just being together again in the familiar surroundings of the Seamill Hydro where we always prepared for crucial domestic or European ties was an emotional experience which made *Pride of Lions*, the tribute marking the 20th anniversary of the day the European Cup was brought back to Britain for the first time, the highlight of my year. Throughout the pages of this book there are many references to that great team which swept Celtic from the wilderness to world fame. I make no apology for this. Even today, almost 21 years on, I'm often asked what made us so special. Well, for the first time I would like to pay my own personal tribute to those priceless men . . . the men money couldn't buy.

153

RONNIE SIMPSON . . . By the time Ronnie played in Lisbon he was 36 but even then he was the greatest goalkeeper I've ever seen. His anticipation was unbelievable and his reflexes were second to none. Ronnie saved as many shots with his feet as his hands. He had this uncanny knack of sticking out a foot at the last minute to avert disaster. For a relatively small man his agility was amazing but Ronnie's most valued skill was in the one-to-one situation when a striker homed in on goal with only him to beat.

You could never bet against him. Even when big Billy McNeill had been beaten Ronnie refused to flap. Just ask any Rangers player of that era — they rarely got past him. In ten years of playing with him I never ceased to be amazed by Ronnie's reactions. They were razor sharp and this instilled confidence in the rest of us. For a veteran he could put many of today's young keepers to shame.

JIM CRAIG . . . Jim once caused a stir by saying within earshot of Jock Stein that football didn't mean everything to him. This didn't go down well with the Big Man who lived for the game but Jim's honesty was refreshing. He didn't take football too seriously and I think that helped him to handle the pressure. A very solid full-back, Jim's valuable contribution often went unnoticed. He covered up a lot for his full-back partner Tommy Gemmell. Jim, now a dentist and part-time radio commentator, was a quiet character off the park but he had a keen football brain.

TOMMY GEMMELL . . . An extrovert. How else can I describe big Tam? The crowds loved it when this showman tried his favourite scissors kick, usually when we were strolling to victory. Tam wasn't the best defender in the world but he had a lot of skill for a full-back and to cap it all possessed a blockbuster shot which became famous throughout the world after his goal in the European Cup final. Tam is now in insurance.

JOHN CLARK . . . John covered up a multitude of sins around him. He had the unique ability to be in the right place at the right time. John strolled through games and was never flustered because he could read any given situation so accurately. Clarkie was the perfect foil for Billy McNeill. A very intelligent player who was tailor-made for management. John is now in charge at Clyde.

BILLY McNEILL . . . Caesar was the perfect captain. If things were going wrong (a rare event) Billy could lift us off the floor with his determination and will to win. Our skipper wasn't particularly skilful on the ground but he made up for this in the air where he rarely missed a header. A great ambassador for the club, Billy, of course, is now Celtic's manager for the second time.

Another boring wait at an airport. Stevie Chalmers is the team-mate lost in thought.

The Lions roar again.

BOBBY MURDOCH . . . The best right-half Celtic have ever had, I don't care what anyone says. Quite simply a superb player. Bobby's reading of a game from midfield was second to none and his anticipation for the interception was uncanny. When you talk about players with great vision Bobby must be top of the pile. His passing was incredible. He could hit a 70-yard pass straight to a team-mate. And his tackling, well, I've never seen him lose a tackle. Bobby was also the "hard man" of our team. If anybody needed sorting out he was the guy to do it, but not in a malicious way. He looked after me on the park. We had a great understanding. Bobby would brief me about opponents and he gave me a steady supply of the ball. Murdie was also one of my best pals off the park. A very underestimated player whom I cannot say enough about. Truly world-class.

BERTIE AULD . . . Bertie was our midfield general. He kept things ticking over all the time. A cheeky, arrogant player with all the confidence in the world, Bertie made the crowds laugh by trying wee daft things, like feigning to take a free kick by dragging

The good, the bad and the ugly. Those rampant Lions, 20 years on.

one foot over the ball. This infuriated opponents. His experience was also invaluable. Bertie played in Celtic teams of the early 1960s before going to Birmingham. It was an inspired move to bring him back. He made time for himself before hitting pin-sharp passes. Bertie is still one of the biggest extroverts in the game, a man whose appetite for football is undiminished. He proved his worth as a manager with Partick Thistle before moving to Hibs. Bertie is now in charge of Dumbarton. A man famed for an expensive taste in cigars!

STEVIE CHALMERS . . . Stevie will never be forgotten for scoring the winning goal in the European Cup final. A player with exceptional pace and poise but a real workhorse into the bargain. Stevie was one of two Lions who specialised in 40-yard crossfield runs which baffled opponents. This was a ploy which worked thousands of times for Celtic. Stevie would set off on a diagonal run and latch on to a precise pass from Auld or Murdoch. He is still on Celtic's pay-roll as a pools official.

WILLIE WALLACE . . . "Wispy" must have been one of the greatest bargains of all time when he was captured from Hearts for only £30,000. Despite his lack of inches, he was a great target man. Willie could hold the ball up because he had superb close control.

157

Celtic played to his strength by pumping balls into his feet. And he could score goals. Willie was a great leader of the front line and courageous into the bargain. Wispy is now coaching "Down Under" in Australia.

BOBBY LENNOX . . . "Lemon" and I roomed together on trips around the world. I'm surprised he is not in a mental institution by now after putting up with me for so long. He was the other guy who made those dashing 40-yard runs. Bobby was one of the quickest players I've ever seen and as sharp as a button in front of goal. He scored a barrowload of important goals for Celtic and a few for Scotland. Bobby outlasted all other Lions playing for Celtic — a testimony to his fitness. He is still playing an important role at Parkhead running the reserve team. He is a great character and a true friend of mine.

Modesty forbids me from analysing my own ability but, suffice to say, it was easy to play in a team so brimful of talent. And what must not be forgotten is the Lisbon era wasn't just about the 11 men who won the European Cup. Men like John Hughes, Jim Brogan, Davie Cattanach and Willie O'Neill provided invaluable back-up when called upon. "Yogi" in particular knocked in a few valuable goals for the side. A bear of a man with a real soft centre. John was a lovely character. And I can't forget the contributions from goalkeeper John Fallon and striker Joe McBride. John lived in the shadow of Ronnie Simpson most of the time but he rarely let Celtic down. He was a great stop-gap measure. He worked exceptionally well with Ronnie in training and was always eager to improve his technique. I will always remember his bravery in the World Club Championship clash with Racing Club in Argentina when he was called in at the 11th hour after Ronnie had been struck by a missile in the warm-up. John did not flinch and played like a true professional.

Joe was the best striker I had seen when he played at Parkhead. Tragically, injury robbed him of a place in the Lisbon line-up. Naturally Joe was shattered to miss out against Inter Milan but he took the blow bravely. I'm certain only injury stopped him breaking all scoring records at Celtic.

So there it is, my run down on the best team in Celtic's history. And team is the operative word. In ten years together I cannot recall a fight or row between the Lions. The harmony and camaraderie was unique. I salute them all.

Chapter Eighteen
TODAY AT PARADISE

It is appropriate in Celtic's centenary year that one of the great Lisbon Lions is at the helm. Big Billy McNeill was obviously brought back from England at the end of last season by public demand. All the fans I've spoken to are delighted with his return to the fold.

In my era, "Caesar", as the punters loved to call him, always had presence. He won respect without trying. As a captain he was a fair man to play under and I'm sure the present players would say the same about the man as a boss. Billy is steeped in the tradition of the club and even after leaving for Manchester City and Aston Villa, where he had a torrid time with two struggling outfits, I always felt his heart was back where it belonged — in the east end of Glasgow.

Now one of the club's favourite sons has things buzzing again at Parkhead and I'm pleased for him. But I'm afraid I cannot be so complimentary about some others who are, or were, in positions of power at the club I still love so much.

For the life of me I can't understand the inadequacies of the Celtic scouting system. A lot of fans might not know much about him but John Kelman, the chief scout, is a very influential figure at Parkhead. He determines the future for a steady stream of youngsters who are desperate to play in the famous green and white hoops. He was appointed during Billy McNeill's first reign as manager at Celtic Park and now sits in a little office at the club, co-ordinating the six to ten scouts who scour the land for talent.

Well, in my eyes, Celtic's recent scouting record speaks for itself. My estimate would be that around £4 million worth of talent has been lost to the club. You only have to look at the players who have been allowed to slip from Celtic's grasp at one time or another. Celtic watched Mo Johnston when he was at Partick Thistle but didn't fancy him. After Mo made a name for himself down south with Watford, Celtic bought him for about four times the sum they could have had him for during his Firhill days. Frank McAvennie was another who came under Celtic's scouting microscope while he was a St Mirren player but again the blond striker wasn't recommended. Now Frank is playing for his favourite team — and doing a fine job — but it cost Celtic nearly £800,000 to lure him away from West Ham earlier this season.

The catalogue of blunders is staggering. Tommy Boyd, the captain of Motherwell, and Dundee's classy full-back, Tosh McKinlay, were others who slipped through the net while playing for Celtic Boys' Club. Pat Nevin of Chelsea was on an "S" form with Celtic but was released. And one of Scottish football's most precious young talents, John Collins of Hibernian, played for Celtic Boys' Club for four years until he was 15. John used to travel from Galashiels to Glasgow once a week to train and again on Saturdays to play for the Boys' Club. Celtic failed to sign him on an "S" form. When you see how Collins has developed it's a crying shame Celtic missed out.

But far and away the biggest oversight was Joe Miller, now the darling of the Parkhead fans. Joe was with Celtic at an early age but somehow wasn't rated because, apparently, he wasn't strong enough. I certainly saw what the boy had to offer. A few years ago Davie Hay gave me the chance to help Frank Cairney run the under-16s at Parkhead and Joe was a member of that side. Ironically, I thought there was an even better prospect around then in the same team, young Dougie McGuire, but he has still to fulfil his potential. During that season Joe was turning it on for us when all of a sudden Alex Ferguson swooped and took him off to Aberdeen.

Now Fergie obviously knows a future star when he sees one, and his judgement proved spot on. But, in my opinion, it should never have been allowed to happen. Miller should have been signed up to keep wolves from the door. As it turned out Celtic had to look on for a few years as Miller progressed rapidly at Pittodrie and his value rose almost daily. Thankfully, he is now back at Parkhead but again it cost the club a small fortune, around £650,000, to remedy a situation which should have been avoided.

Reflecting on the past.

On a personal level I have no time for the guy who is still Celtic's chief scout — and I think the feeling is mutual.

Nor is any love lost between myself and former assistant manager Frank Connor. I saw Connor working at close quarters at Parkhead during my days in a coaching capacity. Connor was Davie Hay's right-hand man but to me it looked as if he wanted to run the show. The man seemed obsessed with his own importance as a coach. In my opinion, he put Celtic back three or four years. I feel he stifled natural flair in players. I often thought some of them were scared stiff to hold the ball and take a man on in case they got the sharp end of Connor's tongue. He was always bawling and shouting at the youngsters. It certainly wasn't the Celtic way of working. He introduced "one-touch" football during training sessions and had players playing in little boxes. It was totally negative. His systems encouraged youngsters to play like robots and I think we are still seeing his legacy at Parkhead with some of the younger players.

I firmly believe Connor had a great inferiority complex and that he always thought someone was after his job. I felt he gave me the cold shoulder treatment at Parkhead. At the beginning everything was rosy when I was helping Frank Cairney with the under-16s and "S" form signings. But the resentment really started the following year when Davie Hay asked me to give Bobby Lennox a hand running the reserves. I think Connor thought I was moving in on his turf and he hated it. Nothing could have been further from the truth. I wasn't bothered about a permanent position at Parkhead. I was only going in as a figurehead, someone the young lads could relate to and admire in the same way as Bobby Lennox.

The reserves mixed regularly with the first team for five-a-sides. I got involved and the lads loved it when I jinked past a few players and tried to nutmeg the likes of Paul McStay. It was great fun — while it lasted. But a few weeks later there was a meeting of all the coaches and it was suggested I no longer take part in the "fun" fives. Maybe Frank Conner thought some imaginary old boys' network was trying to do him out of a job.

Or maybe he was just jealous. Connor wasn't part of that great Lisbon era. Maybe, deep down, he resented the adulation which the Lions still receive wherever they go. I don't know what was going through his mind but I will never forgive him for making me feel so unwelcome at the club I will love to my dying day.

I think Kelman also did his best to stir up trouble. One day Bobby Lennox and I were talking to him in the foyer at Parkhead. Within seconds of Bobby departing, Celtic's chief scout turned to me and said: "He'll have to go." I was flabbergasted. Here he was slagging off a great personal friend of mine, the guy I roomed with around the world for years, and a man who has done and is still doing a fantastic job for Celtic. I could have punched him but I didn't waste the effort.

It was a horrible time, nothing like the good old days when it was a pleasure to walk in the door at Parkhead.

I walked *out* the door for the last time at the end of a highly successful season in charge of a new under-18 side. Here and now I will reveal the true story behind my departure. From the moment I arrived at Parkhead in a coaching capacity I made a private pact with Davie Hay to keep off the "bevvy". As everyone knows, drinking and football have gone hand in hand for me in the past on a few infamous occasions. I broke my word to Davie, although exaggerated stories he heard from some club personnel did not help my cause. In the end Davie approached me and asked me to leave. His own job was under pressure by this stage and I hold no grudge with him over his course of action. He is still a great pal. I told him I had been considering my position anyway. The internal strife was getting me down so maybe it was a blessing in disguise.

But in saying that I can hold my head up and proudly state that my coaching record at Parkhead was second to none. In my year alongside Frank Cairney with the under-16s we swept the boards in Scotland, winning everything in sight. And, in tandem with Bobby Lennox, I helped the reserves to the league title and the Scottish Cup, narrowly missing out on League Cup glory as well. When Celtic appointed me coach of their new under-18 team the success story continued and we made a clean sweep of honours, winning a big pre-season tournament in Inverness, the League Cup, the League and the Scottish Cup. To cap it all we lifted the BP Cup, seeing off the cream of the country in the process.

In those last two years I combined coaching with an eight to five job on a building site. My boss Frank Lafferty gave me time off to go to Parkhead and in hail, rain or snow I trained the lads, sometimes under one light at Barrowfield. I'm not looking for a medal but it must be remembered that my daily job was hard graft. Sometimes I would be digging drains in pouring rain in places like Kirkcaldy but still made it back for training. Originally, Bobby Murdoch assisted me but, when he departed, Davie Provan — whose career was tragically cut short by illness — stepped in.

I'm sure the under-18 lads who worked with me would vouch for my dedication. Certainly I have had no complaints about setting a bad example from parents. Already Celtic are reaping the rewards from that side with talents like Stuart Balmer, Alex Mathie and Dougal McCarrison tasting first-team action. That first team is, of course, led by Billy McNeill who took over in the wake of one of the most distasteful events I remember in the club's history. I'm talking about the sacking of Davie Hay as manager.

I'm not going to comment on Davie's managerial performance, only to record that he did bring the Premier League title and the Scottish Cup to "Paradise" during his spell in charge. But I must comment on the way his departure was handled or, to be more accurate, mishandled by the club's board. As far as I'm aware Davie was the last man in the world to know he had been booted out. Surely that's wrong. Everyone I've spoken to agrees that Davie was badly treated. Celtic don't do business that way normally and I hope they never do so again.

A lot of what happens from now depends on the present Chairman, Jack McGinn. I must admit he's a character I can't get to the bottom of. I was brought up with the great "Dynasty" of the Kellys and Whites. Both Sir Robert Kelly and Desmond White, as I've said, were men with great presence, just like Jock Stein; I may be crucified for saying this, but Jack McGinn doesn't appear to have that essential aura. Personally speaking, it mystifies me why he is chairman of the club.

He seems to have risen in a short space of time to attain the number one position at Parkhead. About ten years ago he was the editor of the *Celtic View*. Then he became a director and now he's been chairman since September 1986. I would have thought that Jimmy Farrell, the senior director, was a more obvious choice.

Jack McGinn seems to have something against me. When he became a Celtic director I recall shaking his hand and saying: "Well done, Jack. It couldn't have happened to a better person." But years later, when I was taken on by Davie Hay, Jack McGinn shunned me. He was standing in the Parkhead foyer with Desmond White and Tom Devlin when Davie interrupted their chat to say I had officially returned to the fold. Desmond and Tom both congratulated me but Jack remained silent.

Over the years I made long-lasting friendships with men like the late Desmond White and Tom Devlin. Jimmy Farrell is a close friend. And today's young breed of directors Kevin Kelly, Chris White and Tom Grant welcome me with open arms at Parkhead. Groundsman Joe Docherty, Jimmy Kennedy, Jimmy Steele, Doc Fitzsimmons and 'Haysie' do the same. I still fall for the female charms of secretary Irene McDonald, laundry woman Mary Mills and all the girls in the tearoom who have saved my life on countless occasions. They are all valued friends but Jack McGinn is not among that number and the crazy thing is, I don't know why.

I also have clear views on the current playing staff at Parkhead. Let me say right away that Billy McNeill has a very fine squad around him now. You can't really fault it. In captain Roy Aitken, Celtic have a man who is an example to every youngster. His dedication to the club is total and that's great to see in this modern era where freedom of contract tempts players to chase cash all over the globe.

I must give a special mention to a player who has already cropped up in this chapter, Joe Miller. Young Joe is, in my opinion, the biggest single improvement made at Parkhead in many a long year. Without him this season I'm convinced Celtic could have struggled in their Centenary year. The boy just oozes class. His arrival has taken the pressure off the other front men, Frank McAvennie and young Andy Walker — another good prospect. It's awfully difficult for two strikers to do all the donkey work but now they have a wide man to work with.

I like to think Joe is doing the same kind of job that I used to do at Parkhead. I always believed in taking men on and creating openings for strikers. The fans love that direct approach. I could sense the buzz of anticipation that went around the ground when I got the ball. I hope that doesn't sound too arrogant but I always felt the fans were there to be entertained and I had a stage on which to perform. Joe is doing the same and the fans idolise him. The boy has flair. He is a complete individual, an entertainer of the highest order. Like all top-class performers he shows that little bit of arrogance on the park, and make no mistake, that sort of thing is infectious. It spreads confidence throughout the team and that's certainly happening now at Celtic. Miller must take most of the credit. He can become a great hero for Celtic over the next decade. I just hope they can hang on to him.

One player in particular has benefited from Miller's arrival more than most, and that's Paul McStay. He is another extraordinary talent. The boy has the football world at his feet. But I must admit a few seasons ago I thought he was falling into a great big hole. Again I think the blame for this could be laid at Frank Connor's door. He seemed to stifle Paul's natural game to such an extent that the young midfield star became slightly negative. He didn't take enough players on, in my book, and those surging runs were almost non-existent. But, now that Miller is out on the wing and Connor is out the door, I think Paul has more options. He can feed wee Joe in the knowledge that he will make a direct assault on goal.

165

And, let's face it, that is what the game is all about — opening up defences and scoring goals.

The trio I have mentioned at length — Aitken, McStay and Miller — are all products of Celtic Boys' Club, the "factory" which has produced so many stars over the years. Back in 1970 chief scout John Higgins approached Jock Stein with the idea of linking the Boys' Club closer to Celtic FC. It was a masterstroke and the club owes John Higgins a great debt.

The same can be said of Frank Cairney, the general manager of the Boys' Club. Frank, one of my dearest friends, was on the verge of becoming assistant manager of Hamilton Accies when Celtic approached him to run the Boys' Club. He accepted and for the past 17 years has given priceless service to Celtic. The man had a major influence on my career and I'm sure I am not the first or last to say that.

There are many other fine young players at Parkhead nowadays but none can match Charlie Nicholas for class. I've always had a soft spot for Charlie. When Nick was in the reserves at Parkhead one of his best pals was Danny Crainie and I remember taking part in kickabouts with them behind the goals. They loved seeing me show off my ball skills. Charlie went on to become a class act himself. I'm only sorry his career hit a bad patch at Arsenal. Certainly his move to Highbury looks a bad one in hindsight but you can't criticise him for going down south. Charlie wanted a fresh challenge and it rebounded on him. I would have loved to see him return to Celtic but I'm sure he will get right back to the top with Aberdeen. But, like me, Charlie's first love is Celtic.

In this chapter I have criticised certain individuals at the club I still adore. I did not do so lightly and hopefully I've made it clear that everyone is not tarred with the same brush. But I have to stand up and be counted and I'm sure thousands of fans will share my views. And, let's face it, the *fans* are the backbone of the *club*. Without them it would all be meaningless. They have a right to know what's going on.

Chapter Nineteen

YOU'LL NEVER WALK ALONE

There's a cliché in football which says fans are worth a goal of a start to the home team. Well, in Celtic's case I would treble that tally because there's no doubt in my mind that the Parkhead punters are the best in the world.

Throughout this book I have talked about numerous successes for Celtic on the park but these glorious days and nights would have been worthless without the fans. Football is all about pleasing the men and women who fork out their hard-earned cash at the turnstiles. Without them the game couldn't exist. During my era at Parkhead Jock Stein drummed into the players that we had to give our all for the Celtic faithful whose loyalty was, and will always be, an undisputed fact.

My personal relationship with the Celtic support is something I will cherish to my dying day. For 14 years I tried to give them what they wanted — entertainment — and they repaid me a hundred times over with encouragement and kindness.

They were part of a big, happy family and even when I left the "nest" those fantastic fans didn't forget me. In fact in 1976 they crowned my career with Celtic in their own inimitable way. By this time I was a Sheffield United player but my heart was still at Parkhead. On giving me a free transfer a year earlier Celtic had promised me a joint testimonial match with Bobby Lennox and that fact alone kept me going through those dim days at Bramall Lane.

At the end of my first season in England I returned to Scotland

and for the next three weeks trained morning, noon and night in preparation for the last big night of my footballing life . . . 17 May 1976. It was my farewell to the Celtic fans, and nothing was more important, so I punished myself to get into the best possible shape.

Despite all the pressure-pot situations I experienced over the years with Celtic I have never felt as nervous as the night before the testimonial game at Parkhead against star-studded Manchester United. I couldn't bear the thought of letting those marvellous masses down. Thankfully, all the organisation for the match was left in the hands of a splendid committee which included my old friend, lawyer Joe Beltrami. But on the morning of the match I was still very apprehensive.

Keeping with tradition, I met up with Bobby in the afternoon for a pre-match meal at the Virginian Bar in Glasgow. It was a small affair with just a few close friends. From there both of us made our way to Parkhead. I felt like a young schoolboy turning up for a trial with his favourite team.

The night started with an "Old Crocks" seven-a-side match between Lisbon Lions and an International Select refereed by my buddy, comedian Billy Connelly, who noised up the Celtic support by wearing a Rangers scarf. At this point I was in the dressing-room with the rest of the lads trying to keep my nerves under control.

Before the kick-off both teams formed a circle in the centre of the pitch as Bobby and I ran out to a rapturous reception. The warmth that generated from the terracings was overpowering as we waved to the fans, over 50,000 of them. A marvellous little gesture from Kenny Dalglish immediately put me at ease. Kenny gave me the ball straight from the kick-off and I weaved past a United player to thunderous cheers. Every time Bobby or I touched the ball the fans responded. Dalglish was dazzling on the night, grabbing a hat-trick as Celtic swept to a 4-0 win. Wee Bobby capped his special night by netting the other goal. I was delighted with my own performance. The hard work had paid off and I didn't disappoint the paying customers who were the real heroes of the night.

The scenes at the start were nothing to what happened at the final whistle as Bobby and I started a lap of honour. It was an emotional moment for both of us and I could feel a big lump in my throat and tears in the eyes as we ran around the track. At one point I broke away from Bobby, sped over to the "Jungle" which was always my favourite spot, and threw both boots into the crowd. It was the least I could do on a night I will never forget.

Farewell to Paradise. My emotional joint testimonial with Bobby Lennox.

The lads at my local, the Windmill Arms.

In the dressing-room afterwards Bobby turned to me and said: "They gave you some reception, wee man." It was a magnificent gesture by one of the nicest guys in the game. Bobby sensed that the fans had given me an extra special tribute on my return after a year and he wasn't resentful.

Funnily enough, a few months ago I bumped into a complete stranger who had one of my boots from that testimonial night. It was certainly the genuine article because one stud was missing!

To this day I still miss playing in front of Celtic fans. In particular I miss the atmosphere they generated on European Cup nights at Parkhead. Nothing could beat it when 60,000 crammed into the ground to will us to victory — which usually happened in the Lisbon era. I often performed better at night under floodlights. I think it was a mixture of the fans' backing and having more time to prepare during the day.

On those special European nights the fans were certainly worth a few goals of a start because they intimidated most Continental opposition. In Europe supporters are usually quite sedate but at Parkhead the noise generally reached fever pitch.

On the domestic front Celtic never play in empty stadia. The fans travel all over the country through thick and thin and this always ensures a perfect atmosphere. And Celtic followers rarely let the club down by resorting to hooliganism, which also makes them some of the most sporting supporters around. Off the terracings they are just as passionate. And that doesn't just apply to the legions who follow the club in Scotland.

A few years ago I accepted an invitation to be the special guest of the Kearney Celtic Supporters Club at a St Patrick's Day parade in New York. One night myself, Frank Cairney and Jimmy McNally attended a Grand Ball where the guests showered us with kindness. It was one long sing-song, with all the favourite Celtic songs taking a beating. At one point the whole gathering sang *You'll Never Walk Alone* and I had to fight back the tears. The following day fans at an Irish Club in New York repeated the dose, so just before our departure I gave them my own rendering of *You'll Never Walk Alone*.

It was a similar story three years ago when I travelled with Paul McStay and other Celtic players and officials to Belfast on a promotion visit. Hundreds of fans assembled for a rally in a big hall. The place was heaving and the adulation we received was so touching. But after less than an hour we had to be led out a side door for our own safety. We were on the verge of being crushed to death by eager autograph hunters!

Only last year I turned down an offer from some Celtic supporters in Australia who run their own team. The boys were willing to pay for my air ticket and all other expenses in a bid to lure me "Down Under" to play for six weeks. It was a remarkable show of generosity but I had to turn down the request for two reasons. One was my fear of flying. I didn't fancy being up in the air for nearly two days. And the other was that I had just started a new job with ELN Communications which demanded my full attention.

But even now, with my playing days firmly in the past, the fans still associate me with just one club, Celtic — and that's the way I like it. Wherever I go Celtic supporters talk about the Lisbon era. To many it is still a fresh memory. They are proud of the club's tradition and that's refreshing to see. I hope the club can reward them in this special Centenary year by winning the League title and securing a place in the European Cup.

And, make no mistake, that's where Celtic should be every year, competing at the highest possible level. It's the top proving ground

A salute to those wonderful fans.

You'll Never Walk Alone, down at the Royal Oak in Viewpark.

for players and an appropriate treat for fans who are top of their own league. Who knows, maybe one day a modern Celtic team will emulate the men of Lisbon and bring the European Cup back to Parkhead?

I hope to see such a day, but no matter where or how Celtic are playing those loyal fans will always be at their side. Support for the men in green and white jerseys will never diminish. Parents will hand down the Celtic tradition to their children who in turn will pass it on to a new generation. Players and officials will come and go but Celtic's solid support will always be there.

Throughout the pages of this book I have tried to be fair and honest. In doing so I have criticised certain individuals but to Celtic FC I say good luck and happy Centenary. And to every Celtic supporter I say "thank you" and keep up the good work.

That way "You'll Never Walk Alone".

JIMMY JOHNSTONE

Born on 30 September 1944 in Viewpark, Lanarkshire; joined Celtic in October 1961 from Blantyre Celtic (farmed out to latter during 1961/62); San José Earthquake (USA) in June 1975; Sheffield United in November 1975; Dundee during 1977/78 until transferred to Shelbourne FC (Dublin) in November 1977; Elgin City during 1978/79 before finishing career in 1980 with Blantyre Celtic as a reinstated Junior.

CELTIC — appearances (excluding substitutions) and goals in major competitions:

	League	League Cup	Scottish Cup	Europe	Total
1962/63	4 (1)	—	1	—	5 (1)
1963/64	25 (6)	2	4 (2)	7 (2) ECWC	38 (10)
1964/65	24 (1)	10 (3)	1	4 FC	39 (4)
1965/66	32 (9)	8 (1)	7 (1)	7 (3) ECWC	54 (14)
1966/67	25 (13)	10 (1)	5	9 (2) EC	49 (16)
*1967/68	29 (5)	8 (5)	1	2 EC	40 (10)
1968/69	30 (5)	7	6 (2)	5 (2) EC	48 (9)
1969/70	27 (10)	4	4 (1)	9 EC	44 (11)
1970/71	30 (8)	9 (5)	8 (2)	4 (4) EC	51 (19)
1971/72	23 (9)	8 (1)	2	5 EC	38 (10)
1972/73	21 (7)	7 (1)	6 (2)	3 EC	37 (10)
1973/74	13 (3)	7 (1)	2 (1)	6 (3) EC	28 (8)
1974/75	15 (5)	7 (3)	—	2 EC	24 (8)
TOTALS	**298(82)**	**87(21)**	**47(11)**	**63(16)**	**495(130)**

* In 1967/68 he played in Celtic's three matches for the World Club Championship versus Racing Club of Buenos Aires, Argentina.

Notes
1. Details exclude appearances as a substitute.
2. Figures in brackets are goals he scored.
3. Abbreviations: EC = European (Champions) Cup
   FC = Fairs Cities Cup   ECWC = European Cup-Winners Cup

Honours with Celtic (major competitions):

1. *League championship*   Nine championship medals for seasons 1965/66 to 1973/74 inclusive (nine in a row).

2. *Scottish Cup*   Winners medals for 1967, 1971, 1972, 1974, (4); finalist in 1963, 1966, 1970, 1973.

3. *Scottish League Cup*   Winners medals for finals held in 1965/66, 1966/67, 1968/69, 1969/70, 1974/75 (5); finalist in 1964/65, 1970/71, 1971/72, 1972/73, 1973/74.

4. *European (Champions) Cup*   Winners medal for 1967; finalist in 1970.

Sheffield United

	League	FA Cup	League Cup	Total
1975/76	6(1)	1	—	7(1)
1976/77	5(1)	—	—	5(1)
TOTALS	**11(2)**	**1**	—	**12(2)**

Notes:
1. Details exclude appearances as substitute.
2. Figures in brackets are goals scored.

Dundee

	League	Scottish Cup	League Cup	Total
1977/78	2	—	—	2

N.B. Statistics not available for Johnstone's stint at San José Earthquake and his career after leaving Dundee.

JINKY — NOW AND THEN

International Honours:

Junior internationist; two Scottish under-23 appearances; four Scottish League appearances; "capped" 23 times for Scotland at full international level.

Full Internationals (dates refer to **years** in which matches played):

1964 v. Wales, Finland (WCq) — full international debut v. Wales in Scotland's 2-3 defeat at Cardiff on 3 October 1964.
1966 v. England, Wales.
1967 v. USSR, Wales.
1968 v. Austria (WCq).
1969 v. West Germany (2 — both WCq).
1970 v. England, Denmark (ECq)
1971 v. England, Belgium (ECq), Holland, Portugal (ECq).
1972 v. Northern Ireland, England (sub.).
1974 v. Wales, England, Belgium, Norway, East Germany, Spain (ECq) — final appearance for Scotland v. Spain in European Championship qualifier at Hampden on 20 November 1974 (Scotland lost 1-2).

Abbreviations: WCq = World Cup qualifier
ECq = European Championship qualifier

Goals in full internationals:

2 v. England at Hampden, 1966
1 v. West Germany in Hamburg, 1969
1 v. Belgium in Bruges, 1974

4